Betty

Betty
CHRONICLE OF A MOVING LIFE

by Jack Fassett

Graphics by Joy Mermin

CHAPEL HILL
PRESS, INC.

ISBN 978-1-59715-055-2
Library of Congress Catalog Number 2008931022

First Printing

This book is dedicated to Jeffrey, Caleb, David,

William, Darby, and Sylvie, Betty and Jack's

grandchildren, and to Amiodarone, the drug

that has extended their grandmother's life.

CONTENTS

FOREWORD

Over eight years ago, shortly after Betty and I, to be close to daughter Joy and her family in Chapel Hill, North Carolina, moved from our retirement retreat in St. Petersburg, Florida, to Croasdaile Village Retirement Home in Durham, our daughter and her husband encouraged me to record my recollections of my youth and life during the period of the Great Depression. As a consequence, I produced, with Joy doing the word processing of my barely legible handwritten yellow pages, a volume entitled *The Shaping Years: A Memoir of My Youth and Education*, which was published by Xlibris Corporation later in 2000. Through the years, Joy and our younger daughter, Lora, on several occasions had asked their mother about her early experiences, particularly during World War II, and suggested that she record them for the benefit of our grandchildren and later generations. However, Betty was never receptive to doing so. Whether her reluctance was due to not enjoying reliving or revealing events during the war or because she did not enjoy writing was never clearly articulated, but she never has produced even a brief memoir.

This volume constitutes a major expansion of a few modest chapters I began writing in mid-January of 2008 when Betty was admitted to the Heart Center at Duke University Hospital for treatment of a critical heart condition. While alone in Croasdaile Village, I found myself reminiscing about our marriage of over sixty years and about her life in the preceding years. As a result, I decided that, even though I did not have firsthand knowledge of most details of her life prior to our first date at the University of Rochester in 1946, I would try to relate her early story. Each day as I took breaks from visits to her in the hospital, and subsequently in the nursing facility at Croasdaile Village to which she was transferred, I recorded a few more memories. Initially, I entitled the manuscript "Nurse Betty" since nursing was such a major part of her life after she entered nurses' training in 1939. However, I later decided to employ the title "Betty's Shaping Years" because I then thought the narrative had become a close counterpart to my memoir. Obviously, I was not able to record details of Betty's early life as Betty could have done. However, I did endeavor to relate with accuracy the most significant happenings of our lives up to the date Betty and I and our two older children, in 1954, seven years after we were wed, finally moved to our longtime home in North Haven, Connecticut, as nearly from her point of view as I could.

I planned to present my manuscript to Betty as a token of my love on Valentine's Day. Prior to doing so, I showed the draft to Joy and her husband and our son and his wife when they came for my birthday on January 30 and visited Betty in the nursing home. Joy, who had reported regularly to her sister in Seattle about Betty's condition, also described the project to her sister. The result was that our children and their spouses all urged me not to terminate the story in 1954, but to record for them and their children a more complete narrative regarding Betty's entire vigorous life. They pointed out that the demarcation that I felt appropriate in my memoir was not equally appropriate for Betty and convinced me to write additional chapters. In view of the major expansion this entailed, neither the original title, "Nurse Betty," nor "Betty's Shaping Years" was any longer descriptive, and the current title was adopted.

I did present the draft of the early chapters to Betty while she was briefly at home over Valentine's Day, and she stated that she enjoyed reading them. However, she had a few corrections (e.g., I had her mother being one of a family of thirteen and it was actually seventeen), but she did not offer any additional details about the matters I had included or provide any insights as to any happenings I had omitted. Unfortunately, that return home was brief, and she was again in the Heart Center when I began writing the chronicle's concluding chapters, which I have now completed. Betty declined to read those chapters when proffered following her return home after her third admission this year to the Heart Center. She stated that she would rather wait and read the completed work. I rejoice that it now appears that Betty will actually have such an opportunity to read, and no doubt to comment further on, the entire manuscript. I confess that when I first started writing this manuscript, I deeply feared that I was writing an extended epitaph that Betty would never see.

The chapters succeeding the "Nurse Betty" draft of necessity constitute more of a joint marital history than Betty's individual story, but our two lives have not been separable during our long and happy marriage. In fact, the concluding chapters in most respects more resemble an extensive travelogue and a unique medical history than a memoir because those two factors have dominated our lives since my retirement. The word "moving" in the final title of the manuscript was chosen to describe Betty's life since, according to my dictionary, the word encompasses three distinct definitions: to change one's location, to take trips, and a characterization of occurrences that affect one's emotions. It seems to me a most appropriate word to describe Betty's life.

I greatly appreciate Joy's assistance, taking time from her hectic schedule as an ESL teacher in an elementary school, in selecting, scanning, arranging, and captioning the graphics that follow each chapter of the manuscript.

April 22, 2008

≈ 1 ≈

Burgettstown and Pittsburgh, 1921–1943

She was joshingly called an "Irish twin" since she and her older sister were born the same year. Betty just missed being a Christmas baby, being born on December 23, 1921, whereas Mary had arrived the prior January. Their father, William Henry Conrad, but always called "Dutch" by his friends and coworkers, had recently begun his lifetime career for the Pennsylvania Railroad, starting as a fireman and, in due course, progressing to engineer. Dutch had married Blanche Bell in 1919 after his return from service in the trenches of France during World War I. His father's family had immigrated to western Pennsylvania from Germany, and his father operated a tinsmithing business in the railroad and mining community of Burgettstown, not far from the West Virginia border. The large old Conrad home, with an adjacent tinsmithing shop, was located on an unpaved short extension of Burgettstown's Main Street. In its rear, it abutted the railroad mainline between Pittsburgh and Columbus, Ohio. A small stream across the road in front of the house usually contained brownish water as a result of nearby mining operations. Blanche Bell was one of the oldest daughters in a family composed of thirteen children (two sets of twins had not lived) led by another railroadman whose family had emigrated from Scotland. The Bells resided in the neighboring small village of Midway.

As a consequence of being born in the same year, Betty and Mary were classmates throughout their careers in Burgettstown's public schools. Betty's family resided in a smaller and newer residence than her grandparents in a group of homes on a hillside not too far away from the older Conrads. Betty and Mary, and eventually their two younger sisters, Mildred and Lois, walked the modest distance from their home to school each day and returned home each noon for lunch. Whereas Mary was quiet, Betty was the tomboy of the family and enjoyed extracurricular activities. In high school she played on the basketball team and she enjoyed playing baseball or football with a couple of her Bell uncles, whose ages were close to hers, and their friends. She also liked to dance, and sometimes she would hurry her lunch and rush back to the school

1

gym where dancing was scheduled each noon during her high school years. She also developed her love for competitive tennis during her high school years: she managed to get to play on a privately owned court, even though she had to borrow a racquet from one of the owners, by being a frequent observer and volunteering to work on maintenance of the court. Since coal mining was the only major industry in the area, except for the railroad yards, a large proportion of Betty's classmates were children of miners with mostly Eastern European origins.

Upon Betty's and Mary's graduation from Burgettstown High School with the class of 1939, Mary obtained employment in the offices of Westinghouse Electric Company and began commuting by rail each workday to Pittsburgh. Betty, still only seventeen, had other aspirations, but the primary outlets for females in those days were teaching and nursing. Dutch's older maiden sister was a career nurse, and Betty opted to pursue that career and obtained agreement by her parents to send her to nursing school.

As a member of the class of 1942 at the Allegheny General Hospital Nursing School in downtown Pittsburgh, Betty was known as "Baby" since she was the youngest in the close-knit class of forty-four girls who lived, studied, and worked together for three years. Betty was not a large girl, weighing only a little over one hundred pounds and standing only sixty-two inches tall, but she was very active and vivacious. Betty loved the challenges of nursing, enjoyed her classmates, and became lifetime friends with several of them. The routine during the first year of nursing school was rising at seven every morning, having breakfast and an hour or so of floor duty before attending classes the rest of the morning and most of the afternoon. In the second year, the number of classes decreased and the hours of floor duty increased. By the third year, virtually all of the long hours were spent performing supervised floor duties with only a few classroom sessions.

On those few weekends when she was free from nursing duties, Betty rode the railroad, using a family pass that was circulated among family members, to Burgettstown to visit her family. During the three-week vacation allowed the nursing students between their first and second years, Betty also went home to Burgettstown, but she found the period very boring because none of her former school friends any longer were in town: all of the boys had left for military service, and the girls had also departed either to attend college or to find employment. There were few social activities during nursing training, but Betty did get to play tennis a few times with other girls and the beau of one of them who was a good player. After saving five of the dollar allowances her mother sent her periodically during nursing school, Betty finally was able to purchase her own tennis racquet.

By the time Betty graduated, Pearl Harbor had occurred, but she was not yet twenty-one, a requirement for becoming a registered nurse in Pennsylvania, and so she commenced working as a general-duty nurse in Allegheny General Hospital. She finally received her certificate on January 4, 1943, and, later in 1943, having passed her twenty-first birthday, she responded to the vigorous recruiting efforts of the Army Nurse Corps.

She and one of her nursing school classmates, Eleanor Burns, decided to join the army together.

Conrad Homestead, Burgettstown

Mary, Mildred, Blanche, Betty and Lois, 1958

Dutch and Blanche Conrad, 1948

Nursing School, 1942

Class Picture, Allegheny General Hospital School of Nursing, 1942

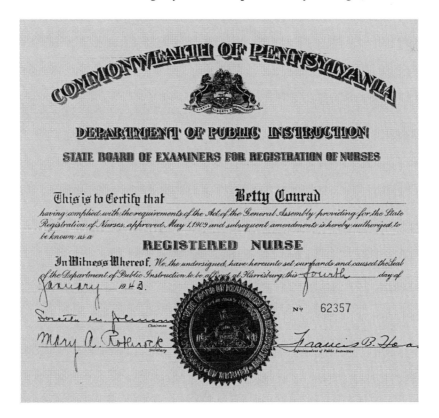

❦ 2 ❦

Tampa and Europe, 1943–1945

The following couple of years were eyeopeners for a young lady who had never been very far from Burgettstown and Pittsburgh. She and her classmate, having taken the oath and been issued their commissions as second lieutenants in Pittsburgh, were immediately sent to the station hospital at Drew Field, Tampa, Florida, for basic training. Upon arrival in Florida, Betty was issued a complete wardrobe of dress, duty and nurses' uniforms, including one of the red-lined blue capes once worn by army nurses. It is certified in her personnel record that she also was issued a gas mask and that she wore it for four consecutive hours during the four weeks of basic training. The training consisted not only of indoctrination to medical practice in the army. The recently instituted program, as described in a brochure entitled "The Army Nurse Corps in World War II," also "stressed Army organization; military customs and courtesies; field sanitation; defense against air, chemical, and mechanical attack; personnel administration; military requisitions and correspondence; and property responsibility." Betty's weeks at Drew Field, however, consisted mostly of long shifts of nursing duty in the Drew Field Hospital which served several air corps training bases in the Tampa area. A popular saying in the hospital was "one a day in Tampa Bay" since there were so many incidents of training aircraft crashing in the bay. One of the nurses training with Betty did have an automobile, so, on a few occasions, Betty got to join a group that traversed the causeway across Tampa Bay for a meal at a restaurant on St. Petersburg Beach. On one occasion, they enjoyed a Spanish dinner at the famous Columbia Restaurant in Ybor City, the center of cigar-making in Florida. Betty also participated in a wedding at a hotel in Tampa when one of the nurses married her hometown beau, a signal corps lieutenant, who was about to leave for a war zone.

Promptly after completion of basic training, Betty, but not classmate Eleanor, received orders to report to Fort Polk, Louisiana. Arriving there, she found that she had been selected to be one of the forty nurses being assembled to become the nursing staff for the newly forming 134th Evacuation Hospital. Such units were somewhat comparable to the MASH units of the Korean War made famous by the long-running TV show. As described in the previously cited brochure, "Within the 'chain of evacuation' established by the Army Medical Department during the war, nurses served under fire in field hospitals and evacuation hospitals, on hospital trains and hospital ships, and as flight nurses on medical transport planes."

Before her new unit departed Louisiana for Camp Kilmer, New Jersey, she was issued an array of heavy winter clothing plus a canteen and mess gear. After only forty-eight hours at Kilmer, the 134th departed on the recently built troopship *Henry T. Gibbons* to join a convoy headed to France. Sharing the vessel were an ambulance company, an engineers maintenance company, a quartermaster company, and, most importantly in view of the status of the European campaign, the 782nd Tank Battalion and its vital equipment. Hindered by poor weather and threats of U-boat attacks, the nervous voyage of the crowded ship took sixteen days. While she did not actually get sick, Betty found the crossing extremely unpleasant and spent most of the crossing in her crowded quarters. The 134th debarked in Le Havre as fierce battles were raging along the front in what became known as the Battle of the Bulge.

Upon debarking, the 388 personnel of the 134th (including 305 enlisted men and 8 administrative officers in addition to the 35 doctors and 40 nurses) were immediately loaded on waiting army trucks for transport to a newly established staging area called Camp Lucky Strike. The *Henry Gibbons* was among a large number of ships to reach the mainland port, and the staging area had been established to receive the influx of fresh troops. As in all of their several subsequent movements across France, Belgium, and Germany, the nurses traveled in the rear of open trucks protected from the weather only by a canvas top. Within hours of settling into their sleeping bags in the cold tents set on frigid ground, the unit unexpectedly got their first taste of the war. When the other units on the *Henry Gibbons* debarked, they were loaded onto a railroad train consisting of WWI-vintage boxcars called 40 and 8s—so named because they were built to accommodate forty men and eight horses. A few hours into their rail journey north, the French trainmen lost control of the speeding engine, causing a derailing of more than forty cars with the engine crashing into the station in a small village. Doctors and nurses of the 134th were roused early in the morning to be transported to the scene and render assistance. Captain Russell Eustice, adjutant of the 134th, some years later wrote a monograph about the terrifying experience ("The Train Wreck at Saint Valery") that described the frustration of the medical personnel upon reaching the grisly scene as follows:

> Military doctors and nurses rushed in from the 134th Evacuation Hospital went right to work, but Captain S. J. Beale, one of our doctors, expressed the frustration of the medical personnel who were without medical equipment or even an aid station in which to operate.

As to the effect of the tragedy on the tank battalion, the monograph quoted one of its officers as follows:

> It was a scene of complete horror, a total shambles. There were just about every conceivable injury among the men who died and the injured: heads snapped off, single and double amputees, much crushing of heads and bodies. Our battalion lost 51 men and 3 officers, with another twelve officers and 116 men hospitalized.

Most of the other units on the train had comparable casualties. It was quite a welcoming to France and the war!

After additional days residing in the tents of the staging area, the personnel of the 134th proceeded in their trucks to a small town, whose name Betty recalls as Remogne and as north of Reims and near the Ardennes, where they set up their hospital in a large old house. Unlike the MASH of TV fame, the 134th was not a stationary operation for a long period. To be close to the rapidly advancing allied front line, which produced most of the casualties, the entire hospital packed up and moved to new commandeered quarters several times during the ensuing months. Rather than always living in tents in open country as did nurse "Hot Lips Houlihan" and her cohorts in *MASH*, Betty and her fellow nurses, who spent most of their waking hours tending to the wounded, usually lived in a variety of urban facilities. Following Remogne, they moved their hospital out of France, and about ten miles into Belgium, to a larger town (population less than ten thousand), Dinant, on the Meuse River and still about one hundred miles from the Rhine. There they occupied a fairly modern school building, but there were no schoolchildren in evidence while they were there.

Since a separate history of the 134th Hospital was never written, it is not easy to pinpoint today the precise locations where the unit was located between its initial deployments and its final combat location in Halle, Germany. However, the previously cited brochure, belatedly produced by the Army Center for Military History many years after the end of WWII, contains some information pertinent to the 134th and similar units. It reported:

The Army Medical Department's newly organized and thus experimental "chain of command" and the nurses' role in it were tested in North Africa and ultimately used successfully in every theater of the war. Critical were mobile field and evacuation hospitals, which closely followed the combat troops. These hospitals were usually set up in tents and were subject to move at short notice. Nurses packed and unpacked these hospitals each time they moved.

It added:

Evacuation hospitals . . . could accommodate up to 750 patients. Doctors operated on patients sent from field hospitals. Patients with postoperative stomach wounds were routinely kept in an evacuation hospital ten days before they were sent on, and those with chest wounds were usually kept at least five days before they were evacuated. Critically wounded patients needing specialized treatment were air evacuated to station and general hospitals. Stable patients requiring a long recuperation were sent via hospital ship.

The brochure cited as an example the experience of an evacuation hospital that arrived in France shortly after the Normandy invasion, months before the 134th, but the discussion is enlightening because their roles were identical:

The 12th Evacuation Hospital deployed to France in July, arriving in Normandy on 1 August. By that time most of the heavy casualties incurred during the first weeks of the invasion had already been evacuated to England....In mid-September the Allies met the German defenses at the Siegfried Line, and casualties mounted. The 12th established operations at Bonneval, where it admitted 1,260 patients in less than one month. It then received orders to deploy to Rheims and operate in the abandoned American Memorial Hospital, which the retreating Germans had left in poor condition. After the nurses spent several days scrubbing and cleaning, they received orders to turn over the American Hospital to another medical unit and to establish an evacuation hospital in a field near the Argonne Forest....The nurses of the 12th moved eleven times in two years. After each relocation they had to prepare a sanitary, comfortable hospital capable of handling large numbers of critically wounded or sick patients. Their experience alternated between periods of exhausting activity and intense boredom. They had to be flexible, innovative, quick-thinking, patient, adaptable, and highly skilled. Their experiences were similar to those of nurses in field and evacuation hospitals everywhere in Europe.

While the unit was in Belgium, a local woman, who had been hired to do laundry for the nurses, invited Betty and a couple of other nurses to her home for a dinner. Food was very scarce for the natives, but the family shared their treasured supply of canned rabbit with the nurses. Also, while in Dinant, a number of the 134th's nurses were sent by truck on detached service to assist at another hospital which was being overwhelmed with casualties. Betty recalled bunking in a really old school building in an unknown village during that assignment.

At the outset, Betty was a general-duty nurse affording whatever type of care was ordered to the casualties before they were returned to duty or transported to one of the general hospitals. Upon joining the 134th, Betty started being addressed as "BJ." The nickname stuck so that, even after the war, all of her army friends still called her BJ rather than Betty. In March 1945, Betty was promoted to first lieutenant and designated a chief nurse. On occasions, the hospital received wounded civilians, including Germans, and at the 134th's final active station, in a former Luftwaffe facility in Halle, Germany, they also treated some Russian soldiers since the Allied forces had met the Russian army at the culmination of its advance through Germany. During the course of their northern trek, the 134th was one of the first units to view the Buchenwald concentration camp not long after its liberation, and Betty was greatly shocked upon seeing all of the various aspects of the inhuman Holocaust. When she first met Jack, she had a number of photographs of conditions at that camp when the 134th arrived, but her album containing them was in a footlocker that was under water when the Fassetts' cellar at Old Orchard Road was flooded in 1973, and they were destroyed.

The previously-cited brochure includes the following comment, which, based on recollections related by Betty, is equally pertinent to the 134th:

After American and British forces repulsed this last German offensive, medical units accompanied the Allied forces into Germany. In newly conquered, hostile territory the nurses experienced new pressures. Third Army nurses noticed that the deeper the Americans went into Germany, the more openly hostile German civilians became. Near Darmstadt, the hospital had to be guarded at all times....

During her months in Europe, Betty established particularly close friendships with two other nurses: Neva "Chick" Morrill from New Hampshire and Peg Lindo from Louisiana. When they received their monthly ration of one bottle of gin and one bottle of scotch whiskey each, they partied together. Since it required only two players, cribbage was a favorite activity of the nurses, and Betty learned to enjoy playing it. On a few occasions, some of the nurses were "commanded" or "volunteered" to don their dress uniforms to accept invitations for eating and sometimes dancing at the temporary officers' club of one of the army divisions they were tailing, but that and other socializing was rare.

In addition to their European Theater Campaign medals, all of the personnel of the 134th were awarded battle stars designated for the Rhineland Campaign and the Central Europe Campaign. Promptly after the European war ended, the 134th was deployed to southern France where its members understood they were going to be transported to the Pacific theater where the war was still raging. The one fringe benefit of their short stay in the south was that some of the officers, including Betty, were granted brief R & R breaks at a facility commandeered by the army in Cannes. Thus she got to relax and take a sailboat ride and a few dips in the picturesque Mediterranean Sea. Photographs taken on that happier occasion show her in a two-piece bathing suit her mother had sent her, an ensemble that she declined to wear thereafter.

The return trip of the 134th to the United States from Marseille was much quicker with no convoy and no threatening U-boats. They arrived at Camp Patrick Henry, Virginia, on September 16, 1945, having been spared a Pacific trip by the dropping of the atomic bombs and Japan's surrender. Discharge from the army at Fort Dix, New Jersey, quickly followed. During their months together, Chick and Betty had both decided that, upon discharge, they would take advantage of the GI Bill and study to become nursing educators. Peg, on the other hand, opted to remain in the Army Nurse Corps, and within a few years she married an army colonel who in due course became a general.

Second Lieutenant, Army Nurse Corps, 1943

Betty at tent

Frivolous Betty

R & R in Cannes

ID Photo

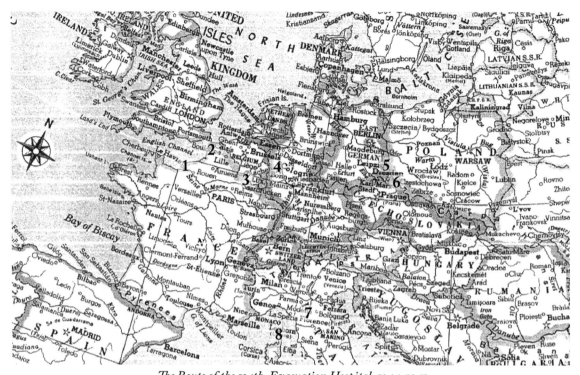

The Route of the 134th Evacuation Hospital, 1944-1945
1. Le Havre   2. SaintValery   3. Remogne   4. Dinant   5. Halle   6. Buchenwald   7. Cannes   8. Marseilles

Betty and Chick Celebrate
Discharge, New York City, 1945

Penacook, Rochester, and Matrimony, 1945–1947

Following discharge, Betty visited her family and friends in Burgettstown and Pittsburgh for a few weeks. Dutch even proposed that she join the local veterans' club, but she had no desire to remain in Pennsylvania and thus adopted Chick's proposal that she join Chick working in the Concord Hospital in New Hampshire while they filed applications to schools that offered degrees in nursing education. Not having anticipated the sudden end to their military service, they had not been able to firm plans for a class starting in 1945 so they were reconciled to waiting until a new class began in 1946. While still in uniform, Chick had dated an air corps officer, Raymond Rapp, who was due to be discharged and to return to the University of Rochester to complete his undergraduate requirements for entering Rochester's medical school in 1947. Finding that Rochester had a respected nursing education degree program, both Chick and Betty applied and were accepted to take two courses during the summer session in 1946 and to begin full-time schedules in September 1946. In the interim, Betty quickly found employment as a general-duty nurse along with Chick in the Concord Hospital. Living with Chick's parents and brother in the small town of Penacook, the two veterans worked, played some tennis, and awaited their return to school.

Before Chick and Betty arrived in Rochester, they were able, through the housing office at the university, to find housing accommodations. They rented separate bedrooms with full privileges to use the kitchen and the living room in a private home on Monroe Avenue also occupied by the daughter of the owners, who were in Florida, and another female tenant. The location was convenient since it was within walking distance to the university's Prince Street Campus (the university then still had separate campuses for men and women) where most of their classes were held. It required a long bus ride, including a transfer, to get to the medical school, which adjoined the River Campus where men were housed and taught. During the six-week summer term, the two veterans took courses titled Educational Programs in Schools of Nursing and Development of Social Concepts in Nursing.

Prior to joining the air corps, Ray Rapp had been a member of the Rochester class of 1946 and had been a star end on its freshman football team. Jack Fassett was a defensive linebacker and offensive left guard on the same football squad. Both Ray and Jack were tapped by and, after initiation, became brothers in the Psi Upsilon fraternity in 1942 before they departed for military service. Being from Illinois, before military service, Ray resided in a college dormitory. Although Jack resided in Rochester and began college as a commuter, he moved into a room in the Psi U fraternity house, which was at the head of fraternity quadrangle, shortly after being initiated. After almost three years in the service (six months in the Army Specialized Training Program and the balance in the air corps), Jack returned to the River Campus to complete his undergraduate education (and again to play football for the Yellowjackets) in early August 1946 (football training began four weeks before classes began). Upon his return, Jack again resided in the fraternity house. Early in the fall, he was appointed house manager, so he oversaw the finances and dealt with the couple the alumni directors had hired to serve the members when the house was returned by the navy, which had used it to house members of its V-12 program during the later wartime years. Though concentrating on completing requirements for his admission to the medical school, Ray also returned to the Yellowjackets football squad for the 1946 season and, during that fall, he generally chose to eat dinner at the fraternity house. He and Jack thus resumed their freshman friendship. Chick and Ray had resumed their dating when she arrived for the summer term, and one dinnertime early in the fall Ray asked Jack if he would like a blind date with an attractive nurse. It was still football season (a poor one with the Yellowjackets winning three, losing four, and tying one), and Jack was otherwise overcommitted so he declined. However, the week following the final game of the season in November (a devastating loss to archrival Hobart College), Jack accepted Ray's offer and accompanied him to Monroe Avenue and was introduced to Betty.

Despite the fact that Jack was a New Yorker, having spent most of his growing-up years in Mineola and East Hampton on Long Island, and Betty was a Pennsylvanian, they were immediately compatible. They liked to drink ten-cent beers together at Clifford's Bar, a short distance from Betty's residence. Betty taught Jack to play cribbage, the game she had learned and often played while in the 134th. Jack was already a novice bridge player so they were available to challenge Chick and Ray when he was not tied up with his demanding medical school schedule. Most importantly, Betty and Jack found lots of subjects to talk about, including their courses, and Jack assisted Betty in writing several papers required by her classes, which, during the first full year of the program, were only indirectly related to nursing. They more closely followed the basic requirements for a science degree including a biology course, two psychology courses, a sociology course, and two courses in the English Department (Composition and Introduction to Literature).

After the Christmas break, Ray and Jack splurged and jointly bought a 1936 Pontiac to provide more convenient transportation to Monroe Avenue (city buses stopped running at 1 a.m.). Unfortunately, the car was a clunker, and it ended in a snowbank when the steering failed one Saturday night in February as Betty and Jack were transporting a brother's date to the Rochester railroad station after a party at the fraternity house. Betty was Jack's regular date at a number of fraternity parties that spring, including a memorable one designated a "come as you were" affair. Most everyone came in some version of their former military uniform (Jack wore his air corps wings, patches, and sergeant stripes), but Betty and Chick chose not to wear their uniforms and medals, not wanting to upstage the coed dates.

Betty enjoyed her college classes, but she much preferred the nursing-related subjects. Not having dealt with academic subjects since high school, both Chick and Betty found the required courses in the other areas particularly challenging. Moreover, it was one of those courses that almost was a disaster to her at the midpoint of the first term. A group of nurses were driving on a field trip for one of their psychology courses to a state mental hospital in New York's Finger Lakes region when their vehicle collided with a state highway department truck. Several of the girls, Betty included, were rushed to Geneva Hospital. She was in that hospital for almost a week being treated for injuries to her ribs and clavicle.

Betty rode the railroad, for which her father still provided a railroader's family pass, to Burgettstown over both Christmas and spring breaks. During the former holiday season, Betty and Chick each received greetings from the former colonel who had commanded the 134th, inviting the key hospital personnel to a mini-reunion at his suburban New York City home in New Jersey on a date in March. Since Betty and Jack were already a twosome, plans were made for Chick, Betty, Ray, and Jack to take a weekend railroad trip to attend the event. Many of the doctors, other former officers, and nurses assembled for the gathering at the former commander's residence for an evening of reminiscing, singing around a piano, and bringing each other up to date regarding civilian life. Jack volunteered to tend the bar and had a good time conversing with the 134th's several versions of Nurse Hot Lips. While Chick and Ray toured the city the day after the party, Betty and Jack rode the New Haven Railroad to Stamford, Connecticut, and she met Jack's parents and sisters and enjoyed a prime-rib Sunday dinner.

Prior to the end of the university's spring term, Jack purchased another clunker, a 1937 Chevrolet. At the time of the New York trip, Chick and Ray announced that they planned to wed in New Hampshire in June, and Chick requested Betty to be her attendant. Accordingly, immediately after Jack's last class in early June, Betty and Jack set off in the Chevrolet for a weeklong visit with Jack's family in Stamford and then to Penacook for the nuptials. Chick's parents housed Betty and Jack until the newlyweds returned from a brief honeymoon for a more extended one at a cottage on a small lake not far from Penacook. Betty and Jack joined the newlyweds at the cottage for a joyous week of canoeing, tennis, bridge playing, and friendship. Before Jack left to return to Rochester and a summer job arranged by a Psi U alumnus in the shipping room at General Railway Signal Company, Betty and Jack announced to their friends and families that they planned to be married on the coming August 4. In lieu of an engagement ring, Betty accepted Jack's "diamond of Psi U" fraternity pin as a token of their commitment.

During Jack's return trip to Rochester, the Chevrolet clunker stopped dead near Worcester, Massachusetts, and it was left with a local brother, who had been an initiate when Jack was pledge father, and the trip to Rochester was completed on the railroad. For the next few weeks, Jack commuted to his job at General Railway by bus and spent his spare time handling fraternity problems and preparing for the wedding.

The couple hired by the alumni when the house was returned by the navy, who had spent the past school year cooking and cleaning for the brethren while residing in an apartment in the lower level of the house, were not entirely happy with their positions, and most of the brothers were quite dissatisfied with their performance. The returning prewar brothers had been spoiled by the fine cooking and dedication of a couple lovingly called Mr. and Mrs. B, who had served the fraternity for several years before the war. The Bs had taken wartime factory jobs when the navy took over the house and moved to an apartment in a big residence occupied by their daughter's family on Seneca Parkway, a wide road with an island park in its center, in a choice Rochester residential area. Jack tracked down the Bs, and they were enthusiastic about returning to the Psi U house and campus life. Their Seneca Parkway two-room apartment thus became available to Betty and Jack on their wedding. Betty arrived from New Hampshire in late July to supervise arrangements for the wedding reception that Mrs. B had volunteered to oversee in the fraternity house, to order a wedding cake, and to join Jack in being interviewed by Reverend Cole, the senior priest at the Church of the Ascension, also on Seneca Parkway, who had agreed to marry the two veterans in the chapel of his lovely church. Before the wedding date, Betty stayed with Jack and Etta May Phelan, old friends of Jack's, who resided in suburban Greece. Betty had met the couple when they attended the "come as you were" party, and Jack, a photographic expert employed at Kodak, had taken lots of hilarious photos. Jack Phelan took wedding photos on August 4 and presented a beautiful wedding album to Betty and Jack as a wedding gift.

Betty's sister Mary served as Betty's attendant at the wedding, and Bill Easton, although not a Psi U, a good friend and fellow member of the 1942 Yellowjackets' football team, served as best man. In addition to Mary, Betty's mother and sister Mildred and her husband traveled from Burgettstown for the occasion, and all of Jack's immediate family plus several aunts and cousins also attended. Chick and Ray hurried back to Rochester from New Hampshire to attend, and most of the area brethren were at the reception. It was a joyous occasion with a little jocularity resulting from the fact that a couple of the brothers spiked the contents of one of the punch bowls that was supposed to contain a nonalcoholic beverage. In the early evening, Betty and Jack embarked on a Lake Ontario steamer for a trip through the Thousand Islands and the St. Lawrence River to Montreal for a three-day honeymoon. Jack was due back at his General Railway job, and Betty was due to begin employment as a floor nurse at Genesee Hospital in Rochester, a job she had obtained before the wedding. Both were due again to commence their studies at the university in early September.

University of Rochester yearbook photo
Nursing Education Program, 1946–1947 Class
Betty, front row, 2nd from right
Chick, 2nd row, 4th from right

Nursing Education

Composed of young women who are studying for a B.S. degree, having already completed a nursing course, the group contains many veterans of overseas service with the Army and Navy Nurse Corps. They are fully accredited members of the undergraduate school, but take most of their classes in Catherine Strong Hall.

University of Rochester yearbook photo, Yellow Jacket Football Squad, 1946
Jack, 2nd row, right end
Ray Rapp, 2nd row, third from left

Happy Betty and Jack, Monroe Avenue

Psi U House, University of Rochester

"Come as You Were" party, Psi U House, Spring 1947

August 4, 1947

With Fassetts at Reception

Departing on Lake Ontario

Sailing to Montreal

Touring Montreal

SENECA PARKWAY, 1947–1948

In later years, Betty often remarked to friends that during her first seven years of marriage she had an equal number of nursing jobs and two children while moving ten times. However, none of the jobs were in nursing education, and she was never quite able to complete her education for her degree in that field.

Betty and Jack's year as residents of Seneca Parkway, with its center island of flowering trees, was busy and joyous. At the outset, they had only a few pieces of furniture donated by the Phelans and the parents of Jack's former Psi U roommate, who also lived on the street. But, shortly after their return from Montreal, Betty shopped downtown and ordered a Simmons Hideabed, a desk, and a nine-by-twelve rug, which were promptly delivered and continued as prized possessions of the couple for many years. The newlywed's kitchen was not at all bare because they had received a variety of kitchen utensils as wedding presents, including a twelve-place set of dishes from Jack's former roommate and his parents and a set of pots and pans from Bill Easton's folks. The one former army nurse, other than Chick, who attended the wedding (Betty had attended her wedding in Tampa before joining the 134th) asked Betty what she would like for a wedding present, and from her came a deluxe ironing board.

While commuting by bus to Prince Street for classes, Betty also was employed part-time on the nursing staff at Genesee Hospital. Jack had advised the coach and his teammates that he would not be joining the squad for the 1947 season and, after completing his job at General Railway, he concentrated on a heavy course schedule (twenty-one units instead of the normal fifteen) in an effort to complete the requirements for his degree in one more year. Not being sure what career to follow after Rochester, Jack took enough classes during his return from service in the Political Science, English, and Business Administration departments to claim a major in any of them, but he ultimately opted to take a Poli Sci degree. As a result of several conferences with his favorite Bus Ed professor about his career dilemma, Jack received an offer for a graduate teaching fellowship in that field at the University of Hawaii for the following year. After much discussion, Betty and Jack decided to forego that tempting offer, resulting in a note from the professor stating, "I fully expected you to desert the ranks of the learned and underpaid."

While Betty had to ride the bus to her classes, several of which were conducted in the evening, and to the hospital, Jack was picked up most mornings by Bill Easton, who lived with his parents not too far away and drove to the River Campus every day. Because his schedule differed from Bill's, Jack usually also resorted to bus rides for his return trips. Bill was dating a coed (Wendy, who ultimately became his wife), and the couple on occasion visited Betty and Jack on a Saturday night for a bridge game. Bill's father was a lawyer in a Rochester firm, and Bill already had been accepted for the next class at Harvard Law School. During one bridge game in early 1948, the foursome got into a strange discussion regarding the location of the source of the Hudson and Mohawk rivers, which resulted in the group setting off during spring break in Bill's convertible to find the answer to the question. The several-day trip was facilitated by visits to Jack's aunts in Glens Falls and Gloversville, New York, but the explorers never discovered the precise source. One Sunday in late spring, when Ray was able to take a break from his medical studies, Bill drove Chick and Ray, Betty and Jack, and Wendy to Niagara Falls for a fast tour of the attraction. It was a first viewing for the Rapps and Fassetts.

Betty also took a few days off during that spring so she and Jack could travel to Burgettstown and he could finally meet her father. In view of the limited time available for the trip, Betty acceded to Jack's suggestion that they splurge by booking a bargain flight on Allegheny Airways (it had not yet become US Air). The flight from Rochester to Pittsburgh, where they were met at the airport, was Betty's first trip by air, and she was a little nervous. Jack, of course, had done considerable flying in the Air Corps and enjoyed flying. It was a pleasant, brief visit, with Dutch welcoming Jack to the Conrad home and as an assistant on the house-painting project which he had started on the old Conrad residence on the extension of Main Street to which Betty's parents had moved when Betty's grandparents passed on. Jack also enjoyed the opportunity to sample many products of Betty's mother's fine baking and cooking skills.

Though most of their time was spent doing work for their studies, Betty and Jack also saw a few movies at the local theater, which was less than a mile distant from Seneca Parkway. One of Jack's aunts resided in a front apartment on their walking route to the theater, and she never forgot seeing the newlyweds rushing by to make the theater's early fifteen-cent admission time with a big bag of home-popped popcorn. Ray's heavy medical school commitments limited socializing with the Rapps, but on a number of Saturday nights one couple would purchase a $2.99 bottle of Gallo red wine and the foursome would have a late-night bridge game with wine cocktails. Early on one such evening, Ray invited Jack to join him in making a quick visit to the medical school where he proceeded to the morgue and displayed the cadaver he was dissecting for anatomy class. Being squeamish about blood, that experience reconfirmed Jack's prior conclusion that he would not be a good candidate for a medical career.

Except for attending classes, neither Betty nor Jack spent much time on their respective campuses during their final year in Rochester. Because of their tight schedules, they saw none of the Yellowjackets' home football games, and they attended only a single Psi U affair during the year. During the spring, Jack spent many hours in the Rush Rhees Library doing extensive research for major theses required by his senior English and Poli Sci courses: one on the history of John of Gaunt, a Shakespearean character, for the Shakespeare course, and one on the background and development of social security programs in the world. A high mark received on the former paper undoubtedly contributed to the surprise Betty and Jack received when they arrived at the Eastman Theater on June 21 for commencement exercises. The printed program disclosed that Jack not only graduated cum laude (despite a mediocre record before military service), but that he was awarded the Caldwell Prize for the most outstanding performance in the English Department.

Having opted not to accept the Hawaiian venture, Betty and Jack were anxious to get on with their lives and perhaps begin raising a family. Accordingly, Jack interviewed with a number of prospective employers during the spring term and accepted a proffered position with Aetna Insurance Company. The Aetna job involved Jack attending the company's school in Hartford, Connecticut, for ten weeks commencing in mid-August, which meant that the newlyweds would have to separate for a period (Betty required one more term of work for her degree) or Betty would have to postpone completion of work toward her goal. She unequivocally opted to go with Jack to Connecticut. Their trip to that state was greatly facilitated by the arrival in May of a check for about three thousand dollars from the lawyer that one of the nurses, also injured in the Finger Lakes accident, had retained to pursue claims against the state for the injuries the girls had sustained. Betty and Jack decided to use the money to purchase a nonclunker automobile and, since it was nearly impossible to obtain a new model in the early postwar years, they turned to Bill Easton who had an uncle in the car business. The uncle promptly produced a sparkling, baby-blue 1947 Plymouth sedan for a fair price. In addition, Jack purchased a hardy trailer and had a trailer hitch installed on the car in anticipation of transporting their recently acquired possessions.

Before loading those possessions on the trailer and heading for Connecticut, Betty completed her work at Genesee Hospital and the couple indulged in a week's vacation. The English prize received upon graduation included a cash gift of one hundred dollars, a windfall that was expended at a Sears store on a camp stove, pup tent, ice chest, and other camping equipment. Jokingly setting their destination as the eastern terminus of Route US 1, the couple drove across Massachusetts, around Boston, through New Hampshire, and well up the coast of Maine. During the adventure, they pitched their tent each night in either a state park or, on the most northern night, in a large field of blueberry bushes. The high point of the frolic was celebrating their first wedding anniversary with a sumptuous lobster dinner at a small inn along the Bay of Maine.

Bill, Wendy, Betty, Ray and Chick at Niagara Falls

Maine trip, 1948; pup tent

Maine trip, Betty on the shore

ENTRANCE UNITS   STUDENT COPY

From ....

Total

THE UNIVERSITY OF ROCHESTER
UNIVERSITY SCHOOL
OF LIBERAL AND APPLIED STUDIES
ROCHESTER, NEW YORK

Record of_____ Betty J. Fassett

Address_____ 31 Division St., Stamford, Conn.

Admitted_____ from _____

           (DATE)   (NAME AND ADDRESS OF INSTITUTION)

Degree Received _ _ _ _ _ _ _ _ _ _ _ _ Date _____

DEPARTMENT AND COURSE NUMBER	DESCRIPTIVE TITLE OF COURSE	1ST TERM GRADE	1ST TERM SEMESTER HOURS	2ND TERM GRADE	2ND TERM SEMESTER HOURS
Summer 1946					
Nurs. Ed. S29	Educational Programs in Schools of Nursing			B	3
Nurs. Ed. S37	Development of Social Concepts in Nursing			B	3
1946-47					
Eng. al-2	English Composition	C		B	6
Soc. al-2	Introduction to Sociology	C		B	6
Biol. al,2	General Biology	C		C	6
Psych. al	Introduction to Psychology	C	3		
Eng. a3,4	Introduction to English and American Literature	D+		C+	6
Psych. a2	Psychology of Learning			C	3
1947-48					
Soc. all1	The Contemporary Family	B	3		
Educ. aD101	History and Principles of Guidance	C	3		
Govt. a3	Comparative Government	C	3		
Nurs. Ed. a9	Supervision in Schools of Nursing	B+	3		
Govt. a4	American Government			C+	3
Educ. aB102	Educational Measurement			B	3
Educ. 122	Principles of Teaching			C+	3
Nurs. Ed. a4	Evaluation of Nursing Procedures			A	3
Summer 1948					
Nurs. Ed. S17	Organization and Administration of Schools of Nursing			B	3

Unless otherwise indicated withdrawal was voluntary

Transcript Issued_____ August 17, 1948 _____

Ruth M. Harper
SECRETARY - REGISTRAR

This transcript requires the official seal of the University to make it valid
(A fee of one dollar will be charged for each additional transcript)
(For explanation of the marking system see reverse side)

Nursing Education course of study, University of Rochester, 1946-1948

≈ 5 ≈

Stamford, Amherst, and Joy, 1948–1949

Betty lived in Stamford with Jack's parents and promptly got a job as a floor nurse at Stamford Hospital while Jack was housed in Hartford in a rooming house retained by Aetna for employees attending school at its nearby impressive home office. During the ten weeks Jack was attending classes and engaging in other activities relating to all aspects of the casualty, surety, accident and health, and fire insurance policies sold by Aetna companies, the Plymouth, together with the trailer and its contents, were garaged in Stamford. Each Friday evening, Jack boarded the New Haven Railroad for the two-hour ride from Hartford to Stamford, returning Sunday evening. Among the couple of dozen students in the Aetna school class were recent college graduates from many locations in the country plus several established employees being trained for promotions. The program left little weekday time for socializing (there was homework), but the students became well acquainted by graduation day. Thereafter, designated as field representatives and given personal business cards, most of the graduates returned to the Aetna branch offices where they had been hired. When the list of assignments was posted in mid-October, Jack and Betty learned that he had been assigned to the Aetna office in Buffalo, New York.

Thus, in late October 1948, Betty, Jack, and their car and trailer of possessions proceeded to the chilly city of Buffalo on the shore of Lake Erie. Following a short period in temporary lodgings, the newcomers, based on good advice from Jack's new boss, signed a one-year lease for a five-room, plus lower-level garage, apartment in a garden apartment development named Allenhurst Gardens in the suburb of Amherst. To fill some of the expanse of the new dwelling—Jack having received a salary increase on completion of school to three thousand dollars a year—Betty and Jack went shopping and purchased a real bedroom set and a dining room table and chairs. Betty's first two planned projects upon getting settled were to determine whether the University of Buffalo, which was located near Allenhurst, offered courses that would permit her to complete the work for her degree and to explore the possible availability of nursing positions in the vicinity. As a result of her inquiries and an interview, she learned that the university did not offer a nursing education program and she was offered a position as a supervisor at one of Buffalo's suburban hospitals. However, both matters shortly became moot (Betty, of course, had to decline the position) when Betty determined that she was pregnant. Betty had apparently conceived during Betty and Jack's second joint visit to Burgettstown, a brief weekend sojourn taken shortly after they moved to Buffalo.

Early in the new year, Ardela, the friendly wife of Jack's boss, gave Betty the name of Doctor Yellen, who she reported was the best obstetrician in Buffalo. When Betty and Jack arrived for their appointment with the doctor and he learned that Betty had been a combat nurse in the 134th, it was like a reunion since, during the war, Colonel Yellen had commanded a hospital unit in Europe and he admired army nurses. Moreover, one of the top nurses from his unit was now the head nurse in the obstetrics division of Buffalo's Children's Hospital. After confirming Betty's pregnancy, Dr. Yellen insisted that Betty keep busy during the pregnancy. He immediately called his friend and arranged for Betty to start to work forthwith as a nurse at Children's Hospital. Driven to work each working morning and picked up late each afternoon by Jack in the Plymouth, Betty spent an enjoyable seven months tending newborn babies. The Fassetts' own firstborn, named Ellen Joy, was delivered by Dr. Yellen at Children's, almost during one of Betty's working shifts since she worked on the day of delivery, August 5, 1949. Joy was a healthy baby.

Life had been quite pleasant at Allenhurst Gardens since most of the Fassetts' neighbors were also young couples. One nearby neighbor had one of the newly marketed TV sets with a twelve-inch screen, and several couples would assemble each Wednesday night to watch the fights and most Saturday nights to watch the *Show of Shows* starring Sid Caesar and Imogene Coca. Jack's Aetna associates were also a sociable crowd so, beginning with a raucous New Year's Eve party at the home of the other older field representative, the couple enjoyed a number of cocktail and dinner invitations. Connie, Jack's older sister, and her fiancé visited in the early summer, which resulted in some revealing photographs of Betty's advanced pregnancy with her overlooking the awe-inspiring Niagara Falls. Betty's condition, of course, precluded any tennis playing by her, but, since ability to play golf was a significant requirement for a successful field representative, and his older cohort had presented him with his extra set of clubs, Betty enjoyed watching Jack hit a few buckets of balls at a suburban driving range on a number of evenings when the weather permitted.

Jack's job involved contacting and assisting Aetna's independent agents in his designated territory and servicing them by doing Aetna Plans for them (detailed analyses of insurance coverage requirements, primarily for larger business clients) as requested. Jack's assigned agencies were in the cities of Jamestown, on the Pennsylvania border; in Niagara Falls; and in many smaller communities including Wilson in the north and Dunkirk in the south. While it was attractive countryside in the spring and summer, the area got very cold with lots of snow coming off of Lake Erie in the winter. On one trip back from Maysville in early February in a blizzard, the Plymouth slid into the rear of another vehicle and then into a snowbank. Since it was not operable and had to be towed back to Buffalo for repairs, the understanding couple who had been tapped, but not damaged, drove Jack to Children's Hospital so he could pick up Betty and arrange for a temporary rental car.

In addition to detesting the weather in Buffalo, and though he liked his boss and associates and Betty was pleased in her new home, Jack found the insurance business unchallenging. His boss, whose wife remained in touch with Betty for the rest of her life, attempted to challenge Jack more by assigning to him the development of Aetna Plans for several industrial insureds not in Jack's territory, but, after extended discussion, Betty and Jack agreed that a different career was desirable and that they both were willing to take the steps necessary to change course. Jack, of course, still had almost two years of college eligibility under the GI Bill.

The law schools of the country had recently developed a Law School Aptitude Test as a nationwide tool for evaluating law school applicants. One of the first such tests was conducted in February 1949, and Jack received permission from his boss to take off the time necessary to take the test. Upon receiving his results (ninety-ninth percentile), Betty and Jack decided that he would apply to Harvard and Yale and, if either was receptive, he would attend law school. The date offered by Yale for an interview in New Haven in response to Jack's application was earlier than the date scheduled by Harvard in Cambridge so Jack made a hasty trip to New Haven in early May. When Jack met with the director of admissions at Yale Law School, she not only offered admission in the ensuing class of 1952, but financial help (half scholarship and half loan) and, by calling the University's housing office, a small apartment in a mansion that had been converted to married students' housing and was only a few blocks from the impressive law school building. At the time, Jack had no knowledge of the fact that prior tenants of the building, Barbara and George Bush and their new baby, had vacated one of the apartments upon the father's undergraduate graduation in 1948.

Probably violating company policy, Jack's boss allowed him to continue to work until September 1 even though the plans for departure had been disclosed. After Labor Day, the trailer—which was again loaded with the Hideabed, desk, and a few other possessions (the new bedroom and dining room furniture was sold)—was once again hitched to the Plymouth and the journey to New Haven with a four-week-old baby was commenced. A last stop in the course of departing was at the office of Dr. Yellen for last examinations of Betty and Joy. The doctor kissed Betty good-bye and lectured Jack not to get so engrossed in law school as to neglect proper care of Betty or the baby. When Jack asked to settle the medical bill, Dr. Yellen finally reluctantly agreed to accept fifty dollars for his valuable services. When Jack handed the doctor fifty dollars in bills, the doctor carefully put the money in Joy's small hand and said farewell.

Field Representative

Allenhurst Garden Apartments, Amherst, New York

HARRY C. JAGOW
PRESIDENT

CLARENCE L. BRAUN
SUPERINTENDENT

DeGraff Memorial Hospital

NORTH TONAWANDA, N. Y.

December 7, 1948

My dear Mrs. Fassett,

    Will it be possible for you to assume your
duties as Obstetrical Supervisor Saturday, January first?

    I feel that you are the person to fill this position,
that you are progressive and that you shall cooperate in improving
the entire department.

                                    Very truly yours,

                                    Anna E. Pfaff

                                    Anna E. Pfaff
                                    Director of Nursing

AEP/f

Job Offer

Betty with Jack and Connie, Niagara Falls, summer 1949

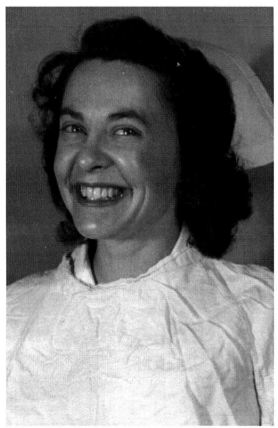

On duty at Children's Hospital, Buffalo

Proud parents off to Yale

New Haven, 1949–1950

The apartment the Fassetts moved into in early September 1949 at 37 Hillhouse Avenue in New Haven was on the second floor of a stately old mansion whose property adjoined a larger fenced lot, also containing an old mansion, which was the home of the president of Yale, A. Whitney Griswold. On the other side was a smaller old home owned by Yale and occupied by the secretary of Yale Corporation. The apartment once had been a dining room with a twelve-foot ceiling, but two narrow rooms had been partitioned on either side to create elongated bedrooms. An impressive wide staircase led from the wide hallway on the first floor, which contained three apartments, to the three apartments on the second floor, and there were also larger apartments in the basement and on the third floor. All of the apartments on the second floor shared the single kitchen and its large refrigerator, and the Fassetts and the couple occupying the other front apartment shared a bathroom located between the units. Most of the couples at 37 Hillhouse had at least one child, but the Fassetts' neighbors were newlyweds. There was a great diversity of graduate, and a couple of undergraduate, programs represented by the occupants, but Jack was the only law student. The first-floor hallway resembled a parking lot as a result of the many carriages, strollers, and tricycles parked along the walls. Hillhouse Avenue was only two blocks long, running from the edge of the main campus to the rapidly developing new engineering and science campus. It was also only two blocks distant from a main bus line that ran the short distance to downtown New Haven and a longer ride to Yale Medical School and Yale–New Haven Hospital. It was a pleasant four-block stroll to the Sterling Law Building. In view of these circumstances, to decrease their expenses, Betty and Jack decided to sell the Plymouth and rely on legs and public transportation.

Within a few weeks of getting established in their new surroundings and determining Jack's schedule of classes and other required law school activities, Betty obtained a position as a floor nurse on the 4 p.m. to 12 midnight shift at the hospital. All of Jack's first-term classes were in required courses, which were scheduled during mornings. Accordingly, it was possible for him to attend classes, do any required library work, and be back at the apartment in time for Betty to don her all-white nurse's uniform and take the bus to work. Betty generally took sandwiches and fruit to work for her evening meal, but sometimes she splurged and had a meal in the hospital cafeteria. Betty had planned also to ride the bus home, but she discovered that the father of the family occupying the third unit on the second floor was a candidate for a doctorate in psychology and his department was housed at the medical school. Fortuitously, the subject of his thesis involved extensive tests using live rats, and each night he had to go to the laboratory and take readings. Since he had a jalopy, timing his lab visits so he could bring Betty home worked out very nicely for most of Betty's working nights.

While Betty worked, Jack did the extensive reading required by first-year law-school courses and tended Joy, including bottle feedings and necessary changings. He became quite adept at rocking the basinet with one leg while also reading a casebook. While Jack was at the law school during the mornings, Betty would take Joy for rides in her carriage around the Yale campus and neighboring areas. With Jack, Betty worried during the first term regarding how he would fare in the competitive environment of Yale after his two intermissions from academia during the war and as a field representative. He was particularly concerned because, among his 144 classmates (consisting of almost equal numbers of other veterans and of students who had either been too young or had otherwise missed military service, plus 7 females) were a number who repeatedly sought in classes to demonstrate their preparation or erudition by volunteering to answer every question posed by a professor, a proclivity not common among veterans who had learned not to volunteer. In any event, Betty joined Jack in celebrating when the results for the first marking period were released, since he was comfortably in eighth position in his class. One consequence was that he was one of the 12 in the class who were invited to compete for election to the board of the *Yale Law Journal,* one of the school's most prestigious honors and, reportedly, the key to employment by one of the top law firms upon graduation. However, from Betty's viewpoint, the consequence was that Jack had to spend more time in the library performing the duties (source-checking materials submitted for publication and, in due course, writing first a "casenote" and then a "comment" worthy of publication) of a *Law Journal* competitor.

There was no tennis and there were very few bridge games during the first law-school year. On a couple of Saturday nights, Betty and Jack did indulge in a game of cards with one of their neighbors, who was attending the School of Architecture, and his wife. There was also no eating out, and Betty sometimes enviously viewed the loin lamb chops or beef filets being grilled in the kitchen by the newlyweds. Betty soon learned that the wife was the sister of a well-known movie actress, Phyllis Thaxter, and, when the petite star sent a large carton of barely worn suits and dresses to her sister, Betty, also being a petite, shared in the windfall. While spaghetti, Spanish rice, stew, and meatloaf were the most common items on the Fassetts' menu, on a few enjoyable occasions, when he was in New Haven on business, Jack's father arrived with a bag of groceries, including a big porterhouse steak. Being very busy and not having a car, Betty, Jack, and Joy went to Stamford for a big meal only a couple of times that year other than for a visit during Christmas break and to attend the wedding of his sister, Connie, and Gunnar Redin, then completing his work at the University of Connecticut for a degree in microbiology. The trip for the wedding was brief since the date coincided with exam period at the law school. However, time was found for taking of a photo showing four generations since Jack's grandfather, David Darby, had traveled from East Hampton to attend the wedding.

Two developments during the second term bode well for the Fassetts' second year of law school. First, toward the end of the second term, one of Jack's professors, Addison Mueller, offered Jack a job, part-time during the balance of the term and full-time during the summer, assisting him with research and, specifically, in the writing of a book in his primary field, contract law. The prospect of enhanced income, even though the going rate for student assistants to law professors was one dollar per hour, made it possible for Betty to cut back on her work at the hospital and to spend more evenings in the apartment. Second, toward the end of the term, the Yale Housing Office inquired whether the Fassetts would be interested in moving at the end of the term to the larger third-floor apartment that was being vacated. Since it was an appealing unit with its own kitchen and bathroom, the offer was quickly accepted. As soon as the new apartment became available, Betty obtained permission to repaint the unit and went to a paint store and purchased two gallons of bright-colored latex paint. In short order, wielding their rollers, Betty and Jack had the new apartment looking bright and colorful for their expected tenancy during the ensuing two years.

Although it intruded on his *Journal* work, Jack enjoyed working for Professor Mueller, and his multiple activities did not preclude his advancing two places in class standing when marks for the first year were released. With classes adjourned, Jack particularly enjoyed eating lunch many days with Professor Mueller and three other professors who remained at the school working on summer projects. Betty and Jack's reverie received a severe jolt when, only a few days after the commencement of hostilities in Korea in mid-June, a telegram addressed to Lieutenant John D. Fassett was delivered to 37 Hillhouse Avenue. It directed the startled second lieutenant (Jack had received the reserve commission at the end of his WWII service) to report within a matter of days to the local army reserve center to join the 729th Railway Operating Battalion, a reserve unit sponsored by the New Haven Railroad, of which Jack had never heard, which had been recalled to active duty because of the Korean crisis, to fill a vacancy for an administrative officer.

Views from outside 37 Hillhouse Avenue
ABOVE: *Jack and Joy showing their apartment building*
LEFT: *Betty and Joy looking toward Yale president's residence*

Christmas Card, 1949

*Four generations
at Connie and Gunnar's Wedding
January 30, 1950*

$\backsim 7 \backsim$

NEWPORT NEWS AND JACKIE, 1950–1951

Since Jack's pleas to avoid his recall (WWII service, a child, law school, inactive reservist, no experience with 729th) fell upon deaf ears (he was told he was lucky getting in early for the new war), Betty and Jack had to do a lot of scurrying during the week the 729th was activated in New Haven prior to departing by rail to the training center of the Army Transportation Corps at Fort Eustis, Virginia. Betty gave notice of leaving to the hospital, a truck was hired to carry the Hideabed and desk and other possessions to Jack's parents' apartment in Stamford, and his parents rearranged the living arrangements for themselves and Jack's younger sister, who still resided with them, to make room for Betty and Joy. The development caused consternation to Professor Mueller and Jack's other lunchmates with the result that the law school admission office reopened its admissions for the ensuing term on the assumption that there would be other military-related losses. That course resulted in the class of 1953 being the largest in the school's history. Despite that initial semi-panic, the Korean War did not seriously impact attendance at graduate schools.

Within days of the arrival of the unit at Fort Eustis, based on a reporting by the unit's executive officer to people he knew in base headquarters of Jack's "legal" credentials, Jack was transferred out of the 729th and reassigned to a position as trial judge advocate in the legal office at headquarters. As a result, Jack's fourteen-month second tour in the army was not the unpleasant experience Betty and he had anticipated. He spent his days prosecuting special (and a few general) courts-martial, conducting investigations requested by the top command, and writing reports of survey regarding lost or damaged military property, all of which functions he found to be interesting and sometimes challenging. Most importantly, as a staff officer (shortly promoted to first lieutenant), he was permitted to live off-base and, with the assistance of his new boss, Major Reagan, a middle-aged Tennessee lawyer who had opted to stay in the service after his WWII tour, he was able to find and rent a nice furnished two-bedroom apartment in a new development in Newport

News called Warwick Gardens, which was about twenty miles from the base. On a weekend pass, Jack promptly traveled to Stamford, purchased a new 1950 black Chevrolet sedan, and loaded Betty, Joy, and Joy's equipment aboard for the trip to Joy's fourth new home at age just twelve months.

Life for Betty in Newport News was pleasant but stressful. The reason for the stress was that, shortly after her arrival in the South, she found that she was again pregnant, obviously having conceived in the hectic days after Jack received his recall order. Betty was examined and scheduled for medical checkups at the base hospital at Fort Eustis and, when it shortly appeared, early in the pregnancy, that a miscarriage was threatened, she was ordered by the army doctor to spend a lot of her time in bed and to avoid exertion. With the assistance of Major Reagan's motherly wife, who had resided in their Warwick Gardens apartment since the development had opened, Betty was able to employ a sunny, young local girl named Daisy to help her care for Joy and the apartment while Jack was on the base.

Army service during late 1950 and the first part of 1951 was considerably different from service during WWII. While the base fast became inundated with recalled reserve units (not only railroad units, but trucking, and stevedore units) being retrained and shipped to the war zone, and a few of the base's career personnel also shipped out, most of the personnel—officers and enlisted men and women—who were career soldiers continued to follow the routines of a peacetime army. There were Saturday night dances at the Officers' Club each week, full troop reviews one Saturday each month, for which Jack had to don sidearms and march with the headquarters group, and frequent inspection tours of various base operations. In view of her condition, Betty was an infrequent visitor to the base, but she was able to eat a dinner at the Officers' Club on one occasion during the Christmas festivities. Also during those holidays, Jack's parents and younger sister drove to Newport News for a visit, but Betty's contacts with her own family were solely through the postal service.

The wife of a neighbor, also an officer on the base, usually drove Betty to monthly visits to her attending doctor at the base hospital. She introduced Betty to the existence, on base and at the nearby military facility at Fort Monroe, of thrift shops. Since Jack had been recalled with a very limited wardrobe of military gear, Betty purchased for him a number of items of apparel including a fine short-coat that was still in good shape when worn throughout prep school by their son. Since Fort Monroe at Old Point Comfort had a better commissary and a better PX than were available at Fort Eustis, the wives also generally did their other shopping at that base, where they were welcomed as military wives. After Jackie was born, the Fassetts were able to take a few short visits on weekends in the new Chevrolet to some of the historic sights of the area, including Williamsburg and the Yorktown battle site.

Flashy automobiles were a fetish with regular army personnel (probably because they had no real home on which to tinker), and every Sunday morning a number of officers residing at Warwick Gardens would be in front of their apartments vigorously washing and waxing their vehicles. However, many manifestations of the transformation of the army from peacetime to wartime status were emerging. One disturbing example for Jack was the escalating number of AWOL, desertion, and self-maiming cases he was called on to prosecute in special courts-martial against enlisted personnel scheduled to be sent to Korea.

Effective in June 1950, Congress had enacted a new, comprehensive Code of Military Justice for the Armed Forces, and a directive was issued requiring each enlisted man or woman to take a four-hour course and each officer to take a ten-hour course regarding it. Jack was designated by headquarters to present the series of courses to base personnel and, although the army provided outlines for such presentations, he spent considerable time polishing them and emulating some of his law school professors. As a result of that activity and of his emerging reputation as a speedy but fair prosecutor, a rumor traveled around the base and Warwick Gardens that Jack was actually a West Point officer assigned to the corps, and not all efforts to squelch the rumor were successful.

After the major miscarriage scare, Betty's pregnancy progressed smoothly until the evening of March 21, 1951, when, upon arriving home, Jack had to rapidly return to the base with Betty for the anticipated event. Betty had made arrangements with Daisy and Mrs. Reagan to care for Joy during her absence. After a few hours of labor, John David Fassett Jr., whom Betty insisted on calling Jackie until he was a big boy and objected, was delivered by an army doctor hastily summoned from an affair at the Officers' Club. Jackie was a healthy baby, but, in accordance with army procedures, he and his mother remained in the Fort Eustis Hospital for a week after he was born. The total cost to the Fassetts for doctors and hospitalization for their second offspring was twelve dollars.

As time approached for the new fall term to begin at Yale, Jack sought a meeting with the commanding officer of the training base to explain his strong desire not to fall another year behind his law school class. The general was understanding, and, although he made a pitch for Jack to consider staying and making the military his career, he had papers prepared for Jack to carry to the headquarters of the Transportation Corps in Arlington, Virginia, recommending that Jack be returned to inactive reserve status. Since that headquarters had already heard of Jack's situation by a communication from the Connecticut congressman representing Stamford who had been contacted by Jack's mother, orders were rapidly finalized and, by Labor Day, Betty, Joy, Jackie, and a relieved lieutenant, following a warm sendoff by the legal office staff and Mrs. Reagan, were on their way back to New Haven. Jack took along a bottle of fine old scotch whiskey that was delivered to him by a young sergeant who had run afoul of military rules and had been ordered to be court-martialed. Jack had convinced the three-officer court to give the sergeant a second chance. Although Daisy begged to be brought along to Connecticut, Betty had to explain to her that a law student could not afford even such devoted help.

Joy at Warwick Gardens Apartments

In uniform for Fort Eustis monthly review

Admiring the new Chevrolet

U. S. ARMY HOSPITAL

Fort Eustis, Virginia

Baby _Fassett_ .... Date of Birth _21 March_ ....

Birth Weight _6–11 3/4_ Weight on Discharge _6–10 3/4_ Length...............

FEEDINGS AND SCHEDULE

Formula:

Milk {Evaporated} .... _1 3_ ....ounces
{Lactum}

Dextri-Maltose No. _Karo_ ...._2_....level tablespoonfuls

Boiled Water .... _17_ ....ounces

Mix and divide into...............bottles of...............ounces each.

Hours to Feed:

Feed at ....

Water: Infant may be offered sterile water once or twice daily between feedings. Refusal of water is quite common, except during summer months, and need not be urged. A glance at the formula will demonstrate that no extra water is needed.

INSTRUCTIONS FOR CARE OF BABY

Bathing and Care of Skin:

Sponge bathe daily. No tub baths until infant is three weeks old. After bath, apply mineral oil to buttocks, folds of legs and folds of arms. If skin is dry apply oil to entire body. Oil, especially in warm weather, may produce a mild skin rash. If such occurs omit oil bathing for 2-3 days.

Care of Cord and Navel:

The cord usually falls off 7-10 days after birth. The cord may remain on as long as three weeks. If cord is still on when baby leaves hospital, apply a square of gauze or cotton, moisten with alcohol and cover with a band. After the cord falls off, drop 3-5 drops of alcohol twice a day over the navel for five days. Continue to cover area with band. The navel usually is dry at the age of three weeks. The belly band can then be thrown away or saved for the next baby!

Care of Circumcision:

If baby has been circumcised clean circumcision each day with mineral oil until it heals. Diaper areas should be washed and oiled each time napkin is changed. Retract foreskin gently at bath time.

Check-Up:

Baby should be seen for check-up at one month of age. Please call for ~~of~~ ~~fice~~ appointment when you arrive home from the hospital.

Clinic   (Over)

eff. 380

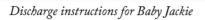

Discharge instructions for Baby Jackie

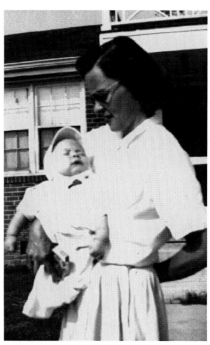

Betty with Jackie

Joy and Daisy

ARMORYVILLE 1951–1953

Betty's second twenty-one-month residency in New Haven during Jack's last two years in law school was different than her earlier brief stay in the Elm City in many respects. Of course, the addition of Jackie to the family was a major development, resulting in more demands for attention, more diapers to be washed and dried (disposables had not yet become the norm), more bottles to be prepared, and more visits to the pediatrician. Probably the greatest change, however, resulted from the fact that, when the Yale Housing Office was notified of the Fassetts' imminent return, there was no vacancy available at 37 Hillhouse Avenue. As another larger effort to handle the influx of married veterans after WWII, Yale had also constructed, using surplus Quonset buildings obtained from the military, in a field behind the Yale Armory and across the street from Yale Bowl and its main parking lot on the outskirts of New Haven, a community called Armoryville, which was capable of housing over one hundred families. There were four rows of Quonsets, one end of each Quonset facing a turnaround driveway, extending from the rear of the Armory to an athletic practice field at the base of a steep incline. Other athletic fields and a playground (containing slides, swings, and sandboxes) erected by Yale for the many youngsters of the village adjoined the Quonsets. Each Quonset contained two units entering from opposite ends, and each unit consisted of one main room for living and cooking, a small bathroom with a metal shower stall, and two cramped bedrooms. A potbellied stove shared the living area to provide heat. Tenants were provided with coal scuttles and a supply of coal in outside bins. There were ample clotheslines spanning posts between the buildings. Promptly upon their arrival in New Haven, Betty and family moved into the interior unit in the right row furthest from the Armory.

In view of the new location, retention of the black Chevrolet was critical, and that created a major change for the Fassetts during their second New Haven sojourn. Betty had not learned to drive during her early or wartime years, but Jack began teaching her how to operate a gear-shift vehicle in the Plymouth and she received her operator's license driving the black Chevrolet so she could commute to any nursing employment and make shopping and medical trips as required. Since Armoryville was several miles from the main campus, Jack also had to commute to his classes and other commitments every day. Having a car, the young family also developed the routine of driving to Stamford quite often on Sundays to eat a good meal and afford the grandparents an opportunity to enjoy their grandchildren.

Jack's class assignments during the final two years, unlike the first year, were not all during mornings, and, in addition, shortly after his return, he was offered a position as research assistant to Professor Ralph Brown, which entailed spending many hours in university libraries (Professor Mueller had departed Yale to the University of Florida during Jack's absence). With Professor Brown, Jack authored a number of articles regarding governmental loyalty and security programs, then a hot civil liberties topic, which were published in law journals. The professor was working on a treatise on that subject with a grant from a foundation which allowed him to pay Jack two dollars an hour, double the going law-school assistant's rate. Another benefit to Jack of working for Professor Brown was that he allowed his assistant to use detailed research he had done for the project to write an article regarding similar programs by private employers. The article fulfilled Jack's responsibility as a *Yale Law Journal* competitor to produce a "comment" for publication in the *Journal*. As a result, Jack was elected an editor of the *Journal* at the end of his second year.

With transportation available, and in view of Jack's new schedule, Betty decided, after becoming settled in Armoryville, that, while she wished to resume nursing, she would try a different aspect of the profession than she had during the Fassetts' prior residence in New Haven. She decided to register with a private-duty nursing registry and accept postsurgical patients in Yale–New Haven Hospital, a role similar to her army nursing, for which there was heavy demand. Under the arrangement, Betty agreed, within reasonable limits, to accept an assigned patient when she notified the registry of her availability, and remain with that patient as long as required, whether a few days or a few weeks. Circumstances dictated that she again opt to work the evening shift, which meant that Jack had to arrive back at the Quonset by shortly after three so she could don her starched white uniform, drive to the hospital, park, and get to the patient's hospital room in time to relieve the day-shift nurse and receive her instructions from that nurse or the attending surgeon. Betty took her evening meal of sandwiches and fruit, which she ate on the job (she consumed a lot of Velveeta cheese), and returned to the Quonset shortly after midnight. It was very demanding when Betty had a case, but she found the practice interesting and sometimes challenging. Many of the cases that Betty treated during this period had received brain surgery, since lobotomies and other brain operations were then being performed at Yale–New Haven for some mental conditions. Betty got to know most of the eminent Yale surgeons and many of the other hospital personnel. The major advantage of working through the registry was that Betty was able to take cases only when she desired and she was able to "sign out" for a number of days or weeks when needed for a rest or other factors deemed that course desirable.

Each afternoon after Betty departed for the hospital, Jack would put Jackie in the carriage and Joy on her stroller and cruise the Armoryville neighborhood, including visiting the playground or watching a football or soccer practice. The prime objective was to insure that the children, after having their dinners, would sleep soundly so that he could return to his books. If the weather was inclement or they were still frisky after their stroll, on a number of occasions they were placed in a little water in the deep kitchen sink or in the shower so they could play under the stream of water and they loved both activities. During the cold winter months, it was necessary to stoke the potbellied stove often, but there was no way to regulate the temperature, and it was usually either too hot or too cold in the confined round-roofed Quonset. Through the winter, the dozens of diapers that Betty washed regularly would often freeze on the clothesline and have to be retrieved in rigid condition. Yale provided several coin-operated washing and drying machines for the Armoryville tenants in a room in the Armory, but Betty preferred the diapers to be air-dried. During these two years, Jack became quite adept at ironing Betty's starched nurse's uniforms on the ironing board Betty's friend from the army had provided as a wedding gift.

Professor Brown, his wife, and two young daughters resided in a modern dwelling on a rocky promontory overlooking Long Island Sound in Guilford, Connecticut. During the Fassetts' first summer back in New Haven, the professor and his wife wished to take a vacation without their children so he offered Jack and Betty the use of their house for a couple of weeks in exchange for Betty's taking care of their girls along with Joy and Jackie. With lovely facilities, swimming in the beach at the base of the rocks, and fabulous views, it was an interesting and pleasant summer vacation for the Fassetts despite the added responsibilities.

Betty and Jack had much more social life in Armoryville than they had had at 37 Hillhouse Avenue despite having an additional child. Quonset neighbors included a number of medical school students and interns as well as a number of doctoral candidates in other fields. There were also two other law school families, one from Jack's original class and the other also from the class of 1953. Some couple from the Quonsets was always looking for an evening bridge game, and during Betty's interludes between nursing assignments, she and Jack managed to do some playing, mostly with a medical intern from Wisconsin and his wife. Despite having limited time for fraternizing at the law school, Jack was named to membership in Phi Delta Phi, a legal fraternity, and, during one sunny day in the final year, the Fassett family attended a daylong picnic of the group at a "farm" owned by the parents of one member in Bristol, Connecticut. While the men played softball, Joy, Jackie, and a few other offspring, supervised by their mothers, explored the grounds and had a good time.

The months flew by during the return to New Haven, and even prior to the holidays of 1952, Betty and Jack were giving serious consideration to where they would like to live and work after graduation. Since Jack had done well in his studies, earning top grades in all of his courses since joining the class of 1953, many options were presented. He made many of the law school interviews scheduled by the placement office, including a lengthy one with a deputy to new Attorney General Brownell (as a result of which he received an offer, which he declined), and he accepted invitations for subsidized visits to two law firms in New York City and firms in Cleveland and Cincinnati, Ohio, and Milwaukee, Wisconsin. Jack received an unusual salary offer from one of the Cleveland firms and one from the Cincinnati firm, where he particularly liked Bob Taft Jr. who was his host in that city, but life in the Midwest did not really appeal to either Betty or Jack. He was impressed by the New York firms, particularly by being ushered in for a long conversation with John

W. Davis, the former presidential candidate, at one of them, but, having been raised in a village of railroad commuters on Long Island, the prospect of that as a career was not very appealing. At the time, Jack was not aware that Attorney Davis was representing South Carolina in its school segregation case pending before the Supreme Court and that the wily advocate knew that Yale's dean had recommended Jack for a clerkship at that court.

In the end, after much discussion, Betty and Jack decided that, even though it was difficult to resist more attractive financial offers, they preferred to raise their children in a less populous area. Jack had also received offers from firms in Hartford and New Haven and by February 1, 1953, he had accepted the Hartford offer. Determined to be settled by the time Joy was ready for preschool, on several Sundays in early February, Betty, Jack, and the kids made the short trip to Hartford to examine, with a real estate agent, residences in Hartford's western suburbs that might be available for them. In due course, an attractive and feasible ranch-style house in West Hartford was found, and Jack signed an offer to purchase and made the required deposit. On the return trip to Armoryville, as they discussed their major decision, Betty posed the question of what would happen if Jack actually got the recommended clerkship about which he had heard nothing since the dean, a couple of months previously, had advised him of his recommendation. In the mail the following day, Jack received a letter from Justice Stanley Reed inviting him to come to Washington to discuss being his lead clerk for the 1953 term of the Supreme Court of the United States. Since such positions are the highest award any law school student can receive, neither Betty nor Jack had any doubts about welcoming the opportunity, even though it meant disrupting their carefully formulated plans. The Hartford firm applauded Jack's award, released him from his commitment, and obtained for him the return of his real estate deposit.

Being accompanied in the audience by Joy, a precocious almost-four-year-old, made it different, but, for Betty, some aspects of the Yale Law School graduation ceremony on June 6, 1953, were reminiscent of the graduation ceremony in Rochester five years earlier. At the Yale event, Betty and Jack first learned that his degree was awarded cum laude, that he had won the Edwin D. Robbins prize for highest grades on annual examinations during his three years of law school, and that he had become a member of the Order of the Coif, the law school honorary scholastic society. A memorable incident occurred during the ceremony when the first female member of the class stepped forward to receive her degree from the dean. A small but loud voice heard by many in the audience, including two federal Appeals Court judges seated a few rows away (Chief Judge Charles Clark and Judge Jerome Frank, both in attendance since they were visiting lecturers at the school), exclaimed, "Who ever heard of a lady lawyer?" Betty was somewhat embarrassed, but the judges and others thought the event was hilarious, and both Betty and Joy can chuckle about it now. Since one of the fellow residents of Joy's tower dormitory while she attended Wellesley College, who is also a Yale Law School graduate, is at the time of this writing a leading candidate for the office of president of the United States, the event is particularly amusing.

Joy and Jackie at Center Square in Armoryville

Betty in uniform for evening shift

At outside playground in Armoryville

Favorite inside playground in Quonset hut

Outside our Quonset

Quonset huts in winter

Christmas in Stamford, 1952

Christmas Card, 1952

Professor Brown's shore home   *Joy with Professor Brown's girls*

SILVER SPRING, 1953–1954

Since Justice Reed wished Jack to arrive promptly after graduation to begin his clerkship and to receive his indoctrination for the position from the lead clerk during the 1952 term, the Fassett family departed Armoryville for the nation's capital on the evening of the last day of the Connecticut bar exam, which Jack took (and was informed, six weeks later, that he had passed). Arriving for his first day at the Court in mid-June, he found the justices surprisingly were still in session, having scheduled a special term to hear a motion seeking a stay of the scheduled executions of Ethel and Julius Rosenberg. After a brief meeting with Chief Justice Vinson, who signed Jack's appointment, and being officially sworn in by the clerk of the Court, Jack was given an indoctrination tour of the facilities and assigned his personal parking space in the basement of the Supreme Court building. He then had a long conversation with Justice Reed (including both instructions and several project assignments regarding the pending school segregation cases) before the justice departed for the duration of the Court's summer recess. The recently wed lead 1952 term clerk also anxiously departed after a few days of offering instructions and advice, so much of Jack's indoctrination was left to Helen Gaylord, the justice's most-capable, longtime secretary (who became a friend to Betty and Jack for the rest of her life), until she departed for her annual monthlong Cape Cod vacation after July 4.

Leaving the children in Stamford for a May weekend, Betty and Jack had driven to Washington and, after some searching, found and signed a lease for a two-bedroom, furnished, ground-level apartment in a large, recently constructed, garden-apartment development on Northhampton Drive off New Hampshire Avenue in Silver Spring, Maryland. Betty had originally hoped that they could find suitable accommodations in the capital's Virginia suburbs, but the management of the comparable garden-apartment development there insisted that a family with two children of different sexes rent a three-bedroom unit, an extravagance the Fassetts rejected. The Silver Spring development proved to be an ideal location for Joy and Jackie since there were many other children (the ground-level apartment in the building next to the Fassetts was a three-bedroom unit housing a patent office lawyer, his wife, and six young children), the grounds contained play areas, and adjacent to the development was a wooded gorge with a small stream and a hiking trail.

Betty gave serious consideration to resuming her nursing career shortly after becoming settled, and she seriously pondered an offer to be a supervising nurse at a nursing home located near Silver Spring, but she had to concede that further pursuit of her profession was not feasible with two youngsters and a husband who worked outrageously long hours. That Betty actually considered accepting the night-shift position at the Eastern Star Nursing Home is confirmed by the fact that the Fassetts' 1953 federal tax return discloses she was paid $206 for the few trial shifts she worked.

Six days each week, Jack left the Silver Spring apartment shortly after 7:00 a.m. in order to be sure to be in his office at the chambers prior to the arrival of Justice Reed. He did not leave at the end of any day until the justice departed for his apartment at the nearby Mayflower Hotel, which was usually around 6 p.m., being transported in his Chrysler driven by his messenger, Ross (a longtime employee from the justice's hometown of Maysville, Kentucky), who also served as the Reeds' general factotum. One advantage of Jack's schedule was that he was able to accomplish the several-mile commutes on New Hampshire Avenue at times of very light traffic. Betty always fed Joy and Jackie and had them in their pajamas and ready for bed when Jack arrived in the evening. Often they were allowed to watch a children's show on the Fassetts' new TV set, their first of many. When Jack arrived, he and Betty had a quiet dinner during which he would often relate the interesting developments of the day. Instead of watching TV, he then usually would sink into an easy chair to read Court papers that he brought home in his briefcase. Jack did not often go to the courthouse on Sunday, but on a couple of occasions he took Betty and the children for tours of the facility and on one occasion he brought Joy in on a Saturday, to the delight of the justice, who had not been expected that day, Helen, and Ross. While the Fassetts on Sundays did take a few hikes in the gorge, a few rides into the city to see the sights, and one trip to see the locks of the Potomac and the trail that Justice Douglas liked to hike, there was mostly work with no bridge playing or tennis games during the entire Silver Spring sojourn.

Only a few times during the 1953 term (a Court period commencing in early October and usually ending in early June) were the Fassetts able to accept cocktail or dinner invitations from fellow law clerks (only a few of whom were also married, but none with children) or other Yale friends practicing in Washington. One exception was made when Jack's fellow Reed clerk, George Mickum, who arrived in late August upon completing a clerkship with an appeals court judge, and his new wife issued an invitation to dinner at their new Bethesda apartment. Another exception occurred when an invitation was delivered to Jack at the Court by Justice Douglas's secretary to a cocktail party at that justice's Washington home on a Saturday night. The invite was assumed to have come because Bill Douglas was an old friend of the Yale dean who had recommended Jack for his clerkship, so Betty found a sitter and they went, but they did not stay long since it was a crowded affair with nobody Jack recognized in attendance. Washington being a magnet for sightseers, the Fassetts enjoyed visits during the year from Jack's parents and Mary Lee, Connie and

Gunnar, Betty's parents, her sister Mary, and, as quite a surprise, Russell Eustice, who had been adjutant of the 134th Evacuation Hospital in Europe.

The major social event of the clerkship for Betty and Jack, however, began when they received in the mail an engraved invitation stating that "The President and Mrs. Eisenhower request the pleasure of the company of Mr. and Mrs. Fassett at a reception to be held at the White House Tuesday evening, December the first at nine o'clock." Starting his first term, Ike and Mamie had decided to reinstate a pre-WWII custom of an annual presidential reception for the justices and their wives, and all of the law clerks were also invited to the event. In eager anticipation, Betty went shopping at the G. Fox Department Store in Silver Spring and found a lovely blue gown and long white gloves for the occasion. Jack and his fellow clerks had to rent formal white-tie-and-tails outfits to be properly attired. A neighbor sat with Joy and Jackie while Betty and Jack had the thrill of going through a reception line and shaking hands with Ike and Mamie. The thrill was increased by the fact that Mamie chose to delay the line to engage in a short conversation with Betty. Attending the White House affair compensated Betty in part for not having been able to attend the state funeral in the National Cathedral after Chief Justice Vinson suddenly died just as the new Court term was to begin. At that event, Jack sat in the third row behind Justice Reed (who, as second senior justice, was one seat in from the center aisle; the Vinson family occupied the first row), diagonally across the aisle from the row in which were seated the President and Mamie, Vice President Nixon and his wife, and former President Harry Truman. Jack got to meet and converse with Truman the following day when he came to the Court to visit his appointees and old friends, Justices Minton, Burton, and Clark.

Not being a veteran, Justice Reed's second clerk (each justice was authorized to hire two), was somewhat younger than Jack. He and his bride, who had only recently completed college, were natives of the Washington area and thus there was no issue about where he would practice at the completion of the term. Betty and Jack, on the other hand, were again faced with a dilemma about their future. Both clerks and both wives were invited to a cocktail party given by the Reeds for all of the justice's law clerks to celebrate his sixteenth anniversary on the Court. At that occasion, Betty got to meet Harold Leventhal (a judge on the federal Court of Appeals), Phil Graham (publisher of the *Washington Post*), and their wives; two of the justice's earliest clerks; plus most of the other former clerks, who mostly practiced in Washington or New York, and their spouses. Near the end of the 1953 term, Mrs. Reed again invited the justice's current clerks to their Mayflower apartment for a quieter dinner and conversation, and it was a pleasant affair.

While the Supreme Court is always in the limelight, the 1953 term received exceptional attention from both media and public for two major reasons: first was Vinson's death with an extended period of speculation regarding who would be named by the president to be his successor; second was the pendency of, and on May 17 the decisions in, the cases challenging segregation by race in public schools. Whereas Jack got to meet and know Vinson's successor, Earl Warren, Betty never had an opportunity to meet the charming man. From his first day as a clerk until the day he departed the Court, Jack was deeply involved with aspects of the segregation litigation as he related in later years in his memoir, in several articles published by the Supreme Court Historical Society, and in *New Deal Justice: The Life of Stanley Reed of Kentucky* published in 1994.

Despite the press of work, during the Court's spring recess, the Fassetts managed to take a brief vacation with their children. It was the first of many camping trips Betty and Jack would take with Joy and Jackie. They proceeded down the Skyline Drive and spent the two nights of the venture in Shenandoah National Park, with the children sleeping in the car and Betty and Jack in their pup tent. In addition to hiking a trail in the park, they left the Skyline Drive to visit Monticello, Ash Lawn (President Monroe's home), and the campus of the University of Virginia.

As the term of the Court progressed, Betty and Jack began to give serious attention to the next step in their lives. Many former law clerks, often as a step toward appointment to a judicial position, choose to serve for a few years at the Department of Justice or at one of the government agencies. Jack was approached by a representative of the department as well as by the general counsel of the Securities Commission about positions, and Betty and Jack actually spent a few weekend hours looking at homes and investigating school conditions in Washington's Maryland suburbs. While Betty saw available houses she liked, not only in Bethesda, but in the more rural suburbs of Potomac and Olney, she decided that their prior decision, to work and live in Connecticut, was a good one.

During the term, Jack was visited in his office in the justice's chambers by Bob Taft Jr. from the firm that had offered him a position in Cincinnati and by young partners from the Jones Day law firm in Cleveland and the Davis Polk firm in New York with new proposals. The partner from Wiggin & Dana, the relatively small New Haven firm that was general counsel to Yale University, who had interviewed Jack a year earlier, also visited and made an offer that Betty and Jack decided to accept. While the financial terms merely continued the salary Jack was being paid as a clerk (fifty-two hundred dollars annually), that amount substantially exceeded the going starting pay for new associates hired by law firms in Connecticut. Betty correctly felt that the cost of living in New Haven would be considerably less than in Washington, New York, Cleveland, or Cincinnati, and she was convinced that the quality of life for children and parents would be superior in the Elm City.

Toward the end of the term, Joy developed a case of infected tonsils and Betty chose to have her hospitalized in the nearest hospital to the apartment, a Seventh-Day Adventist hospital in Takoma Park. Betty was able to stay in the hospital with Joy, then approaching five years of age, during the tonsillectomy and her few days of hospital recovery. Jackie enjoyed the fact that, on one of those days, he accompanied his father to work and received much attention not only from Helen and Ross but also from the amused justice. Joy always thereafter remembered the meals she was served in the hospital because no meat was ever served and she had never before eaten a "green hamburger."

Once the decision was made to return to Connecticut, Betty and Jack were anxious to obtain housing there near a good elementary school prior to Joy's start of kindergarten. In early June, Betty and the children took a trip on the Baltimore and Ohio Railroad from Silver Spring to visit her family in Burgettstown. Upon their return, with the apartment lease expiring at the end of June, and with the Court adjourned and the justice gone on his summer visits, Jack drove the family to Stamford. His parents entertained their grandchildren while he and Betty went to New Haven to explore the housing possibilities. Luckily, after viewing a number of homes in New Haven's northern suburbs of Hamden and North Haven, Betty and Jack found precisely what they desired in a development of six three-bedroom split-level houses on lots slightly larger than an acre, each being constructed by a local contractor at the junction of Ridge Road and Bishop Street in North Haven. North Haven was a fast-growing village of about ten thousand residents with an excellent elementary school system. It did not yet have a high school, but one was planned. A couple of the houses in the small development were completed and occupied and three of the remaining four were sold, leaving 92 Bishop Street, a steeply sloping lot across from an open field that had once been farmed and bordered in its rear by a deep wooded glen. The wooded glen had once contained a Girl Scout camp, imaginatively called Fairy Glen. Jack signed a purchase agreement, using the same deposit money he had used over a year earlier in West Hartford, and also executed a mortgage-loan application that the builder avowed would be processed and approved quickly in view of Jack's job at Wiggin & Dana, which was legal counsel to several of the local banks. The builder promised to expedite construction so that the house could be occupied by Labor Day, prior to the start of the school year at Ridge Road Elementary School, about a mile distant from the property.

Betty and the children stayed in Stamford until the house was available, minus landscaping and a few details, when promised. Jack was committed to being available at the justice's chambers to indoctrinate the two successor clerks (George Mickum departed for a job at a Washington law firm shortly after adjournment), so it was necessary that he find sleeping quarters in Washington. Initially, pursuant to the hospitality of Helen Gaylord, Jack occupied the guest bedroom in the home she shared with her sister (and he enjoyed many meals with the interesting, maiden-lady, career government employees). When the sisters departed for their annual Cape Cod vacation, he spent the remainder of his clerkship residing in Justice Reed's office, using his comfortable couch for a bed, enjoying the shower in the large bathroom, and eating most meals in the Court's public cafeteria.

Jackie in front of Silver Spring apartments   *On the doorstep with Grandma and Grandpa Conrad*

Joy and Jackie with friends in front of apartment on Northhampton Drive, Silver Spring, Maryland 1953

First Fassett TV at Christmas, 1953

Joy and Jackie visiting the Supreme Court

Visiting the zoo with Connie

With Grandma and Grandpa Fassett

First Fassett family camping trip

Betty and Jack dressed for White House reception

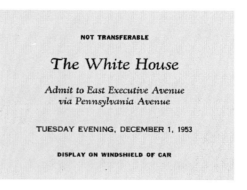

Invitation and parking permit
for White House reception

	DIAL		DIAL
Dixon, Frank SC Rm 33................	342	Hallam, H. C. Jr. SC Rm 314...........	314
Dodson, George A. SC Rm 114...,......	281	Hamilton, Charles L. AO Rm 54.........	397
Dooley, Charles L. SC Rm 304A........	347	Hamilton, Everett E. SC Rm 33.........	342
Douglas, Mrs. Elsie L. SC Rm 138......	245	Hampton, McQueen SC Rm 33...........	342
DOUGLAS, William O. Assoc. Justice Rm		Harding, Raymond E. SC Rm 114........	283
106	235	Hardisty, Mrs. Margaret M. AO Rm 210.,	429
Drake, Lucian D. AO Rm 22D...........	371	Harrison, Hansford SC Rm 114..........	281
Duplicating, AO Rm 22D...............	392	Hartley, Earl L. GPO Rm B39..........	318
Dybrack, Miss Theresa M. AO Rm 212...	431	Hathcock, Frank B. SC Rm 33..........	342
Dynamo Room, SC rm B1..............	353	Hawkins, Albert N. SC Rm 33..........	342
		Hayes, N. Harry SC Rm 35..............	327
E		Hayes, Miss Vivian E. SC Rm 29........	351
Edmonson, George R. AO Rm 54........	397	Heard, Elbert E. SC Rm 35.............	327
Electrical Shop, SC Rm B8.............	297	Heckman, Robert C. AO Rm 214........	401
Elevator Mechanic, SC Rm B8..........	297	Hefner, Carroll A. AO Rm 22D.........	375
Emery, Marcus E. GPO Rm B39.........	318	Higbie, Robert E. SC Rm 241..........	305
Emmons, George A. SC Rm 350........	311	Hodge, Miss Nancy J. AO Rm 231.......	410
Engineer's Office, SC Rm B8............	297	Hood, Olyus F. SC Rm 118.............	252
Evans, Edward J. SC Rm 35............	327	Hoppe, John H. AO Rm 202............	446
Evjen, Victor H. AO Rm 22.............	405	Hornsby, George R. SC Rm 258.........	320
		Horowitz, Bernard AO Rm 256..........	452
F		Houser, Mrs. Ellen R. AO Rm 22A.......	378
Fajella, Walter T. SC Rm 35............	327	Houston, G. Richard SC Rm 350........	311
Fan Room #1, SC......................	356	Hudon, Edward G. SC Rm 330.........	316
Fassett, John D. SC Rm 122............	227	Hughes, John F. AO Rm 10A...........	388
Feary, William J. SC Rm B-8..........	297	Hutchinson, George E. SC Rm 114.......	259
Finnan, Miss Anne M. SC Rm 241.......	305	Hutchison, Henry M. SC Rm B8........	297
FIRST AID, Rm 6.....................	340		
Flynn, Richard J. SC Rm 130A.........	215	**I**	
Fondersmith, Mrs. Elva H. AO Rm 22D...	375	Iannucelli, Anthony AO Rm 214..........	401
Fowler, Miss Mary W. SC Rm 259.......	293		
FRANKFURTER, Felix Assoc. Justice Rm		**J**	
131	231	Jackson, Leo SC Rm 4.................	269
Freeman, Guy SC Rm B8..............	297	JACKSON, Robert H. Assoc. Justice Rm	
Freeman, Orville H. SC Rm 33..........	342	138	245
Fry, Eugene N. SC Rm 102.............	278	Jackson, Royal E. AO Rm 10...........	441
Funk, Mrs. Mary M. AO Rm 10B........	388	Jacobs, Walter P. SC Rm 35............	327
		Jacoby, Robert M. SC Rm 7.............	349
G		Johnson, J. Fred AO Rm 54............	397
Gaither, Lewis L. SC Rm 35............	327	Johnstone, James Jr. AO Rm 216........	455
Garabedian, Edward V. AO Rm 214......	403	Joice, W. Harold SC Rm 41............	343
Garner, Morris W. SC Rm 33...........	342	Jones, Miss Braney L. SC Rm 219........	322
Gayaut, Philip U. SC Rm 219..........	323	Jones, C. L. SC Rm B8................	297
Gaylord, Miss Helen K. SC Rm 120.....	226	Jones, Elmer D. SC Rm 114............	281
Geeslin, Ernest L. AO Rm 10...........	443	Jones, Melvin C. SC Rm 33............	342
Giancoli, George SC Rm B41...........	345	Justices' Conference Room SC Rm 128....	219
Gibney, Miss Edith C. AO Rm 231.......	382	Justices' Dining Room SC Rm 239.......	346
Godfrey, Tiffney C. SC Rm 35..........	327	Justices' Library SC Rm 241............	305
Graff, Mrs. Helen D. AO Rm 214........	403		
Gray, Herbert Jr. SC Rm 33............	342	**K**	
Greene, Miss Elizabeth C. SC 152A.......	218	Kelly, Miss Frances A. SC Rm 118........	252
Gregory, Collie W. SC Rm 33...........	342	Kendrick, John AO Rm 256.............	452
Gronlund, G. Raymond SC Rm B41......	345	Kendrick, John B. SC Rm 35...........	327
Gymnasium	292	Kenney, Edgar L. SC Rm 128..........	219
		Kimmel, Kenneth C. AO Rm 22B.......	365
H		Kitchen, Mrs. Flora L. AO Rm 10A......	388
Hackl, Frank R. SC Rm 35.............	327	Kite, Miss Mary G. SC Rm 219.........	322
Hall, Robert C. SC Rm 35.............	327		

[2]

*Telephone directory,
The Supreme Court,
1953–1954 term*

*Official
parking
permit*

TO
UNITED STATES
SUPREME COURT
GARAGE

EXPIRES _____   **PERMIT NO.** 23

Approved by Metropolitan Police Department

≈ 10 ≈

Bishop Street and Lora, 1954–1963

Betty loved her new home, liked her new neighbors, was pleased with the Ridge Road School, and was challenged by all the projects the new abode entailed. While the other five houses in the development were built according to a typical split-level design, the builder had found it necessary (but did not advise the Fassetts in his rush to completion) to modify the plan for 92 Bishop Street to deal with the steep slope of the lot. This resulted in the lower level, which contained a family room with a bathroom as well as the garage and cellar, being a full flight of stairs instead of just six steps below the main living area. The hasty schedule had not permitted time for landscaping around the dwelling as required by the contract and building permit. The steepness of the lot also led the builder hastily to construct (with red sandstone from the area) retaining walls along the driveway and outside the family room rear door. Otherwise, the abode was sumptuous: a living room with a large brick fireplace and a dining room adjoining the well-closeted kitchen on the main floor with three decent-sized bedrooms and a bathroom six steps up to the upper level, which was above the garage and the family room (with a large void between the upper floor and the ceilings of the lowest level due to the design change). The builder sheepishly avowed that the design change, which was made at his expense, was not only necessary but considered a substantial enhancement by the building inspector.

The Fassetts moved in immediately after the formal transfer of title from the builder, once again moving their Hideabed, desk, and few other possessions from Stamford where they had been since Jack's recall by the army. No sooner had the eager new homeowners moved in than they were greeted by one of the hurricanes that periodically hits Connecticut. Thus, they saw much erosion of their unlandscaped yard, found lots of downed branches and leaves, and experienced a day and a night without electricity until the downed lines could be restored.

Promptly after making arrangements for Joy to commence classes at Ridge Road School and to be picked up each school day at the end of the driveway by the school bus, Betty set about her two major initial projects: supplementing the Fassetts' possessions that had been retrieved from Stamford with basic furnishings for the new home; and setting to work taming the large yard. The few shrubs and the small grass area, which the builder soon had installed to meet his requirements, left almost an acre of rugged terrain requiring clearing and Betty began the job with a heavy pick and a stout shovel she purchased at the local Farmers' Coop store. She spent time each day clearing the large side yard of bushes, many cedar trees, and strange roots that she would accumulate in a pile for Jack to burn when he returned from work in the evening. Only after several fires did she and Jack learn that the strange roots were asparagus, since the field had once been an asparagus bed when the area had been farmed. A more disturbing development was their learning that the ancient-looking vines she had pulled from the old apple trees on the border were poison ivy. The lesson was learned when Jack developed a bad case of poison ivy rash from the smoke of the bonfires. In any event, by the summer of 1955, Betty had succeeded not only in clearing most of the side yard, but she had cleared another patch in the rear where she began a vegetable garden containing tomato plants and rows planted with bean and squash seeds.

The new home was indeed countrified. On many mornings during the several years before houses were built in Fairy Glen, the Fassetts would watch deer in their rear yard and see the results of raccoons visiting Betty's garden and the garbage can at the rear entry to the house. During one of Jack's first outings with a new rotary lawn mower purchased to cut the expanding yard, Jack ran over a rabbit's nest containing several babies. And one day, a utility worker, hooking up a line at the front of 92 Bishop Street, killed a large copperhead snake on the Fassetts' front bank.

Shortly after the Fassetts moved in, Betty was contacted by one of Jack's acquaintances and requested to be the solicitor in the Outer Ridge area of North Haven for the Greater New Haven United Fund, the paramount local charitable organization that supported most of the charities in the area. Not having had any prior experience, Betty only reluctantly accepted, but she had an interesting, though time-consuming, experience, usually with Jackie along, calling on the numerous old residents of, and a few recent arrivals in, the neighborhood. Many of the elderly ladies she met, some of whose families had lived in the town for more than two centuries, insisted on serving tea and regaling Betty at length on town and family histories. With Joy in the school system, Betty also began attending the regular meetings of the Parent-Teachers' Association of Ridge Road School and, after three years, of Center Elementary School, when Joy and Jackie were transferred there as a result of a school-realignment plan. Joy loved both of her schools, and Betty was very impressed with the teachers and the principals at both. Being a regular participant, a few years after the children's transfer to Center School, Betty was requested to become president of that school's PTA, a role she was timid about undertaking. However, when Jack agreed to be co-president, she accepted and enjoyed the function while performing all of its duties.

Jack, too, was being tapped for activities in the fast-expanding town. As a typical old New England town, it had a Board of Selectmen and all important matters had to come before town meetings. A neighbor up the Fassetts' street, a former farmer who now operated a successful dairy-delivery business in addition to an ice cream manufacturing plant in town, was the First Selectman. Shortly after the Fassetts moved in, the Selectman rang their front doorbell and delivered a gallon container of delicious fresh peach ice cream and, in the spring, he rang again to deliver a large striped bass that he had caught that day on a fishing trip in Long Island Sound. Within a year of the Fassetts' arrival, the long-time moderator of North Haven's annual town meeting (who subsequently became a close friend to Jack and ultimately the chief justice of Connecticut) was appointed a state trial-court judge. Jack agreed to pinch-hit at the next town meeting, a role that he thereafter performed for many years until the town-meeting form of government was superseded by a more practical form for a town then exceeding twenty thousand residents. The change resulted from state legislation authorizing a Town Charter Revision Commission, of which Jack was chairman, whose recommendation was supported by a final town meeting.

One of the most satisfying aspects of her new home for Betty was the new friendships she developed. Foremost among them were the two couples who had recently moved into the two conventional versions of the builder's model home, located around the corner on Outer Ridge Road, which had been completed first. Dick Barker was a young assistant professor in Yale's engineering school, and he and his wife, Sela, had two young children, a boy and a girl. Bob Hart had recently begun his private medical practice, specializing in internal medicine, in the adjoining town of Hamden. He and his wife, Rusty, had three children: Lee was slightly older than Joy, and Bobby and Kenny were close in age to the Fassetts' offspring. Bob had been raised in New Hampshire, had attended Yale, received his medical degree from Cornell in New York City, and then returned to New Haven for his specialty and to settle down. While at Cornell, he met Rusty, a redheaded nurse raised in a small town in upstate New York. In short order after the Fassetts arrived, a path was beaten by the children and the adults through the rear of the Fassetts' lot to the abutting rear of the Hart's Ridge Road lot. There soon were swing-sets and other play equipment in the Hart, Barker and Fassett rear yards, and all of the neighborhood children rode school buses together to attend North Haven's public schools. As fellow nurses, Rusty and Betty had much in common, and the Fassetts and Harts became close friends. Many times the Fassetts and Harts attended football games at Yale Bowl together and, since Bob was an ardent fisherman, every fall Betty and Jack would join the Harts and some other couple for a fishing trip on a chartered boat in Long Island Sound when the bluefish were "running." One of Betty's favorite fishing memories is of the time she persuaded the charter captain to troll in a different area of the Sound and she landed a sizeable striped bass.

Betty and Jack also had most-friendly relations with the two other Wiggin & Dana associates, who had both been with the firm for a couple of years, and their wives and children. The wives of both couples had deep roots in New Haven although the husbands, both WW II veterans, were not New Haveners and had received their law degrees from Harvard Law School and Columbia Law School. Both couples had purchased homes in North Haven, but in developments closer to the city than the Fassetts'. In short order, a rotating car pool was developed with the driver, when it was John Barnett's or Newt Schenck's turn, having to drive about a mile north to pick up Jack. Betty drove the crew in on Jack's turns (with Jackie along until he started school), and she often returned to pick him up at the end of the day. The three lawyers did not attempt a regular car pool for their return trips because, being a trial lawyer, from the outset, Jack's hours were different from those of the two office lawyers. Moreover, some months before the 1955 Yale University year began, having received permission from the partners of Wiggin & Dana to do so, Jack was invited by Yale to add to his busy schedule teaching courses in the Political Science Department at the University. As a visiting lecturer, he taught a large lecture course in Development of Constitutional Law during the fall term and one in Contemporary Constitutional Law during the spring term, plus evening seminar courses both terms for graduate students. Jack enjoyed and was challenged by teaching, but he got very little sleep either the summer before or during the college year as he prepared lectures and performed other professorial duties. He had to grade all of the tests, but Betty carefully maintained his marking records. Wiggin & Dana generously did not alter Jack's salary during his teaching, and his stipend from Yale enabled Jack to repay his entire law-school loan. However, by graduation in 1956, Jack and Betty had decided that it was impossible both to teach and practice, and Jack was more interested in continuing his career as a trial and appellate lawyer than becoming a full-time faculty member. Jack proudly recalled his short professorial career in 2003 when he received an unanticipated letter addressed to "Professor Fassett" from federal Appeals Court Judge Richard Arnold, whose rumored appointment by President Clinton to the Supreme Court did not occur due to the judge's declining health, who had read one of Jack's articles in a Supreme Court Historical Association publication. The eminent judge wrote to "tell you how great your course was. Constitutional law should be taught historically. Your course was a lot more enjoyable than the class I took in law school . . ." Judge Arnold's obituary appeared in *The New York Times* less than a year thereafter. He was a Harvard Law School graduate.

When Jackie was examined at the start of his schooling in 1956, the examiner discovered a problem with one of his eyes. As a result, Betty took him to ophthalmology specialists who diagnosed a condition necessitating surgery, but the surgery had to be postponed until he grew larger. Accordingly, throughout his early years, in addition to pediatricians, Betty had to take Jackie for regular visits to eye doctors and he had to wear glasses all of the time. Although Betty also made periodic use of her nursing skills by regularly volunteering to serve during Red Cross blood drives in the town (which were frequent because a large Pratt & Whitney plant had been constructed on the east side of town and it had several thousand employees), with both of the children in school all day, she yearned to get back into nursing. When the head of the Visiting Nurse Association approached her in 1957 to become a visiting nurse in the town, she decided to accept the position on a half-day basis as long as it did not interfere with the children's schooling or vacations. During the years that she continued in that job, the duties of which involved calling at the homes of a variety of patients recovering from hospitalizations, suffering illnesses, or just being aged or infirm, she got to know, and to be known by, a broad cross-section of both longtime and recent North Haveners. During the same period, again with his firm's permission, Jack became prosecutor in the town's antiquated Trial Justice Court. The elected trial justice sat for court in the Town Hall one evening every week hearing traffic and criminal cases (the major ones of which were "bound over" to a state trial court), but Jack's position also involved many evening and weekend visits from the town's expanding police force—officers delivering files or seeking advice.

Immediately after getting settled in North Haven, Betty became a member of the United Church of Christ Congregational Church, and she and Rusty were two of the key members of its choir for many years, practicing one night each week and donning their choir robes for two services each Sunday. While Jack chose to attend services only on rare occasions, at the request of the minister he did serve on the church finance committee with Bob Hart. Only Joy regularly attended the church's Sunday school, and she and her mother would usually stop on their way home on Sunday mornings to purchase fresh-baked rolls and buns at the local bakery to treat the delinquent males.

The Fassetts did not take a summer vacation in 1955 since Jack was working on lectures for his constitutional law courses, but they undertook one immediately after Ridge Road School recessed for the summer in June 1956. After a brief visit with Betty's parents in Burgettstown, they proceeded down the Blue Ridge Parkway to a campsite in Cherokee National Forest where they hiked and, using their limited camping gear, gained camping experience. From there, they visited Fontana Dam and then headed south, crossing Georgia into Florida, stopping only in Ocala, to visit Silver Springs and take a ride in a glass-bottom boat, and in Clearwater, where Jack sought to find the tennis club where the pro for whom he had worked in East Hampton in 1941 taught every winter. Suitable campgrounds were scarce as they proceeded down the west coast of Florida and then across the Tamiami Trail so they spent several nights in motels. When they reached Miami Beach, they discovered, it being the dead season for tourists, that they could rent a large motel room with cooking facilities and a large swimming pool one block from the ocean for twenty-five dollars per week. They spent two wonderful weeks at the Duane before hurrying back to North Haven. During the stay at the Duane, to his great pride, Jackie learned to swim underwater and Joy became an able surface swimmer.

Their first Florida vacation was so enjoyable that the following June, without attempting any camping, Betty, Jack, and the children, plus Jack's parents, returned directly to the Duane where they had reserved its best three-room unit for two weeks for fifty dollars per week. The only sightseeing detours attempted on that journey were a trip to Florida's Keys, which was aborted at Homestead because of the intolerable heat in the non-air-conditioned car, and a one-day stay in St. Augustine to tour that historic city's sights en route home. The following year, celebrating Jack having become a partner in his law firm at the start of 1958, Jack fulfilled a promise he had once made to his mother one day to take her west to Yellowstone Park, since she had always treasured a painting of that scenic place, received as a child from an artist spending a summer in her East Hampton home. Betty's mother and father welcomed the carload of Fassetts for a short visit as they headed west, Betty's and Jack's fathers meeting for the first time. Jack's mother kept a detailed diary of the trip which recorded visits to Jewel Cave National Monument, the Black Hills, the Badlands, and, thereafter, stops of several days each at Yellowstone National Park, Grand Teton National Park, and Salt Lake City. At this stop, everyone visited the Mormon Tabernacle, and only Betty, Jack, and the children attempted to swim in the lake, becoming encrusted with salt. Las Vegas, Nevada, and Disneyland in California were also on the itinerary. During the stop in Las Vegas, the elder Fassetts spent an evening in a casino, but children were not admitted so Joy, Jackie, and their parents instead enjoyed their motel swimming pool. Before heading to California, Jack took the group to see Lake Mead, over which he had flown in training during the war, and Boulder Dam. The group stopped for a lunch of cheese sandwiches at a park along the lake where the temperature exceeded one hundred degrees. Jack's mother's log reported that it was the first time she had ever served grilled-cheese sandwiches without use of a grill. A memorable time was had by all, despite the frequent intense heat and the tight quarters in the recently acquired Ford sedan, which still did not have air conditioning. It was so hot crossing Arizona (on Route 66 at the start of the return trip) that a majority voted not to take a sixty-mile side trip to visit the Grand Canyon, but Jack overruled the vote and took the sweating clan to view from its southern rim the wonder he had viewed from the air while in gunnery training in the air corps. Jackie commented that it was "a big hole."

Starting shortly after arriving at Bishop Street, Betty and Jack spent much time adding improvements to their property. After it was cleared and planted with grass, some of it zoysia with which Betty was experimenting, plus one peach tree, the large side yard became a touch-football field for all of the neighborhood children. When the sandstone walls the builder had hastily erected shortly began to crumble, Betty discovered a source for a supply of attractive, but heavy, blue-green igneous rock where a highway contractor was blasting through a ridge while constructing new Interstate Highway 95 in West Haven. She received permission to help herself to chunks of the rock, and she and the children made dozens of trips in the Fassetts' new Ford station wagon hauling all she dared carry each time. Jack became quite an expert at constructing stone walls, employing the rock not only to replace the builder's crumbling walls with higher ones, but to build a long circular wall across the front to border a new turnaround driveway that was carved out and paved. Betty expanded her garden to multiple new annual crops, including a bed of strawberry plants, and a high wire fence was erected around the entire garden in an attempt to thwart the variety of animals from Fairy Glen who continued to enjoy swiping her produce.

Having always had dogs at her home as a child since her father was a hunter, Betty accepted from one of her visiting-nurse patients a frisky puppy of mixed breed who was named White Sox by the children. Jack built a fancy, shingled doghouse for the pet, but to Betty's consternation, since she fed and cared for him, White Sox, immediately upon Jack's arriving home from work each evening, would rush to cuddle on his lap in his recliner. White Sox's tenure only lasted about a year because he learned to chase rabbits throughout the neighborhood, barking loudly, and he swiped a steak from a neighbor's grill one weekend. Betty gave White Sox and the doghouse to a local farmer who was happy to give him a more suitable home.

During the summer of 1959, Betty and Jack undertook the major project of adding a three-room plus bath addition to their home. Jack drew the plans, hired a contractor with a drill to excavate the red sandstone for the foundation, and employed two local freelance carpenters to do the basic construction. After the foundation was poured and awaiting the hardening of the concrete, Betty, Jack, and the children took a shortened vacation in the station wagon to see the St. Lawrence Seaway and the massive Niagara Falls hydroelectric project that was being constructed by the Corps of Engineers. Upon their return, after the carpenters had completed their work finishing the exterior and framing in the interior of the job, Betty became proficient at assisting Jack in installing mahogany paneling and shelving in his new den, pine paneling and window seats under the two large picture windows overlooking Fairy Glen in the rear, and vinyl tiling throughout the addition.

The new family room became the location for what had become weekly Wednesday evening bridge games between the Harts and the Fassetts. Usually on Saturdays and preceded by cocktails, Betty and Rusty alternated in preparing sumptuous dinners preceding bridge contests and conversation that would often last until after midnight. Prior to the Fassetts' arrival at Bishop Street, the Harts had a regular monthly bridge session with another doctor and his nurse-wife. That group was expanded to add the Fassetts and another lawyer (the doctor's brother, who was a partner in a Wiggin & Dana competitor and, it developed, had played football opposite Jack while at DePauw University) and his wife and, shortly, also an insurance agent and an Armstrong Tire Company engineer and their wives, expanding the group to three tables. The group not only rotated monthly meetings for bridge, but, for many years, celebrated every New Year's Eve together and, as each member reached a fortieth birthday (and, subsequently, their fiftieth), passing on an unopened bottle of Geritol that had been presented to Bob as the first to reach that landmark age.

Jack's partner, John Barnett, and his wife, Betsy, who was a member of the old New Haven Sargent family (famous for locks), were members of the New Haven Contract Bridge Club, which claimed to be the oldest duplicate bridge club in the nation. The club met monthly, and the ladies often dressed in gowns for eight tables of serious duplicate bridge. No table talk or posthand discussions were permitted, and the travelers conveying hands between tables were carefully guarded. In 1959, the club, the membership of which, except for the Barnetts, consisted of seniors, decided to add some new members, and the Harts and Fassetts were invited to join. For a couple of years, Betty and Jack enjoyed the Wednesday night sessions, but Jack found it difficult to concentrate on serious bridge when he was in the middle of a trial, and the Fassetts opted to cease their membership.

During the summer of 1960, the addition to the house having been largely completed, and having become somewhat spoiled by having largely abandoned tents for motel rooms on their most recent long trips, the Fassetts again traveled south, relying on motels for accommodations. However, instead of heading back to Florida, this time the destination was New Orleans. En route, educational stops were made at Mammoth Cave National Park in Kentucky, Andrew Jackson's Hermitage, Meriwether Lewis National Monument, Shiloh Battlefield National Park, and several additional Civil War battle sites along the Natchez Trace. In New Orleans, the family wandered Bourbon Street, drove to nearby Chalmette National Historical Park, and Joy and Jackie sat for sketches by an artist in that city's central park famous for its congregation of artists. To this day, those sketches, which were also framed in New Orleans (the frames cost more than the artist's fee), adorn the Fassetts' dining room wall.

After returning from New Orleans, Jack initiated his last major project at 92 Bishop Street. With much help from many of the neighborhood kids who carried red bricks delivered by a North Haven brickyard (one of the town's historic industries) from the Fassetts' front driveway one-by-one to the rear of the new addition, Betty and Jack constructed a large terrace with brick walls and planters and a brick grill outside the new family room. During that winter, Betty used her nursing and parenting skills acting as a substitute mother to the three Hart children, assisting Bob's mother who came for the period, while Bob and Rusty were simultaneously hospitalized for several months to be treated for cases of tuberculosis. Bob's confinement in the VA Hospital in West Haven was extended after they removed one of his lungs, but, fortunately, Rusty's case was less severe.

With young Jack, no longer Jackie at ten years of age, and Joy, almost twelve, Betty and Jack planned a major camping trip to commence immediately after the children's classes recessed in June 1961. No longer willing to rough it in their Sears-purchased pup tent, Betty and Jack purchased an umbrella tent large enough to sleep four (although Joy and Jack had their own pup tents, passed on by their parents) and a kerosene stove to supplement their prior meager equipment. The night after school recessed, the travelers camped at a state park in the Catskills in New York, and the following day, after visiting Old Fort Niagara and observing the changing of the guard, they crossed into Canada. Crossing back into the United States, they then crossed the Mackinac Bridge and camped at a spacious state park on the Upper Peninsula of Michigan. Crossing the Dakotas, they visited Badlands National Park and Theodore Roosevelt National Park and ultimately reached their destination, Two Medicine campground in Glacier National Park, where they pitched their tents for a weeklong stay. While there, they did a lot of hiking (resulting in big blisters on several feet), which led to seeing a great variety of animals in the wild. They found it necessary to eat their dinner during late afternoon each day and then to retire to the big tent to read or play games before bedding down since the sun set early behind the mountains and it got both dark and cold. One morning in early July, they awoke to find that they had to clear four inches of snow to cook their breakfast. On the return trip home, Jack showed the family the campus of the University of Colorado in Boulder and Lowry Field in Denver where he had spent time during his air corps tour.

Having completed all of their planned homestead projects, Betty and Jack planned another long camping trip for the children's summer vacation in 1962. Heading east this time, after a stop to see the Lexington and Concord sights, they camped at Bradbury Mountain State Park in Maine before arriving at that state's Acadia National Park. There, they pitched their tents for several days, tested the frigid waters of the Atlantic Ocean, and all scaled the rocky climb up scenic Cadillac Mountain, before boarding a ferry from Bar Harbor for Nova Scotia. During the seven days they circled Nova Scotia, enjoying visits to the Halifax Citadel, Grand Pre National Historical Park (celebrating Evangeline and the southerners who fled to Nova Scotia at the end of the Civil War), the Fortress at Louisburg, and the Alexander Graham Bell Museum, plus traversing the scenic Cabot Trail, their tents never got dry since it rained intermittently and it was foggy all of the time. They saw none of the view from the Cabot Trail, and they were happy to get back on the mainland at Fundy Provincial Park in New Brunswick where the sun shone for the balance of their vacation. At Fundy, the family enjoyed many days of hiking, playing games, and observing the famous large tidal changes in the Bay of Fundy.

A short time after returning to North Haven, Betty had to sever permanently her arrangement with the Visiting Nurses and terminate her strenuous yard activities since, though well into her forty-first year, she had become pregnant during a rainy night on Nova Scotia. A leading Yale ob-gyn doctor, who was a client of Jack's and had recently moved his family into a new home near the Fassetts, was Betty's doctor. The pregnancy and the delivery went relatively uneventfully. However, Doctor Billings had convinced Jack to bed down on a cot in a doctors' lounge adjoining the delivery room at Yale–New Haven Hospital on April 5, 1963, so he was present at the time of the delivery of the Fassetts' third healthy baby, who was named Lora Jean. It was indeed an exceptional experience to be present for such a major event!

TOP LEFT: *92 Bishop Street, first winter*
TOP RIGHT: *Original sloping back yard*
MIDDLE LEFT: *Rear view after addition with new patio*
MIDDLE RIGHT: *Clearing rear garden*
BOTTOM LEFT: *Joy and Jack with White Sox in front of
   new addition and turn-around wall*
BOTTOM RIGHT: *Playing basketball by new stonewall and
   backboard*

Singing alto in the choir, North Haven Congregational Church

Tailgating with Rusty and Bob Hart at Yale Bowl

Betty catches big striper

*In the swimming pool
at the Duane
Miami Beach, 1957*

*Overlooking the
"Big Hole",
south rim of the
Grand Canyon,
1958*

*Lafayette Park, New Orleans,
1960*

Camping at Two Medicine Lake,
Glacier National Park, 1961

Acadia National Park, 1962:
Rock climbing at the beach
Wading in frozen surf
Scaling Cadillac Mountain

❧11❧

Bishop Street, 1963–1972

Betty and Jack resided at 92 Bishop Street for eighteen years, the longest period of residency for Betty during her life. The nine years there after Lora's arrival were a period of many changes for her and all of the Fassetts. No longer having responsibilities as a Visiting Nurse, for the first time, Betty found herself being just an active mother and housewife for an extended period. Joy, at almost thirteen, was a loving sister who helped with Lora, but looked forward to completing her years at North Haven's Junior High School and entering North Haven High School, which had been built since the Fassetts moved to town and had already produced several classes. Young Jack was twelve, a student at the junior high, awaiting an imminent operation on his eye, and already determined to be a chemist. He grew crystals in containers in his room, and Betty made numerous trips to a chemical supply store in New Haven to purchase requested tubing, chemicals, and other supplies for him. During the summer of 1963, when there was no traveling vacation for the Fassetts, young Jack attended a summer school in town sponsored by Yale where he took three courses, including Latin, a subject in which he later won a national award. He also volunteered that summer as a candystriper at the Yale–New Haven Hospital.

Jack's community activities and law practice were going through transitions. Because of the clear conflict of interests (a bitter strike at all United Aircraft Corporation plants, including the Pratt & Whitney facility in North Haven, in which controversy Jack and his firm were representing the employer), Jack had resigned as town prosecutor, but he was next appointed chairman of the Library Board, which oversaw the operation of the two town libraries. That position led to his being chairman of a committee set up to plan and oversee the construction of a new, larger central library. Betty found it humorous when, at the Annual Policemen's Ball, the major town social event to which the Fassetts were invited each year, the emcee would refer to Jack as one of the "town fathers." The United Aircraft strike also had a major impact on Jack's law practice since, during litigation involving the company's claim for damages caused by illegal union activities during the strike, which litigation finally reached trial status in 1963, Jack's mentor at Wiggin & Dana and the firm's senior litigator died. Jack suddenly inherited the case that was on trial in Hartford for many weeks, but also unexpectedly found himself senior trier in the firm.

During this period, he had been retained to represent the small towns of Connecticut in a legal action brought on behalf of city residents challenging the apportionment of seats in Connecticut's General Assembly (one of the cases leading to the one-man/one-vote decision by the U.S. Supreme Court), and it was anticipated that the United Aircraft case would also be appealed to the nation's highest court. Jack thus took the step in April 1964 of traveling to the capital to be admitted to practice before that Court. Betty and Lora accompanied him, and they were hosted by the Mickums, Jack's 1953-term fellow clerk, at their Bethesda home where they were raising their fast-expanding family of six children. Admission to Supreme Court practice represented the acme of Jack's legal career as a litigator because, although he tried and argued many cases during the following nine years, his primary attention was being diverted to business matters (he was elected to the Board of Directors of New Haven Savings Bank in 1963 and to the board of the publisher of the city's two newspapers in 1967) and legal work for a single client, Wiggin & Dana's largest, United Illuminating Company (UI), the electricity supplier to southern Connecticut.

Jack was on his way home to North Haven from a jury trial in the federal court in Hartford on November 6, 1965, when the lights along Interstate 91 went out when the Northeast Blackout began. When he arrived at Bishop Street, Betty had a roaring fire going in the fireplace where she was warming a dinner for herself and Jack (with Jack's work hours, the children were generally fed before their parents on weekdays) and by the light of which Joy and her brother were doing their homework. The following day, Jack received a request from UI to handle the public hearing that had been summoned by the State Public Utilities Commission to investigate UI's role in the disaster and to prepare to handle expected lawsuits. As recounted at length in *UI: History of an Electric Company—A Saga of Problems, Personalities, and Power Politics*, written by Jack after his retirement, for the ensuing eight years he became progressively even more involved with UI affairs, both business and legal, leading to his being elected to its Board of Directors in April 1972. From Betty's viewpoint, the only advantage of Jack's increasing involvement in utility matters was that Jack's appointment by UI as its representative on the Legal Committee of Edison Electric Institute, the industry trade association, involved annual multiday meetings at luxurious resorts. She thus was able to accompany Jack on trips to Hilton Head Island; Point Clear in Alabama; the Broadmoor in Colorado; Camelback Inn in Scottsdale, Arizona; the Top of the Mark in San Francisco; and the Breakers in Boca Raton, Florida. Since the first four trips conflicted with school schedules, friends or Jack's parents cared for the children, but, for the California meeting, Lora accompanied her parents and they visited Sequoia, Bryce Canyon, and Yosemite national parks before proceeding to the meeting. Little Lora became well known to the lawyers and their wives at the meeting since the general counsel of Long Island Lighting Company persuaded her to sing "Do-Re-Mi" for the group at one informal dinner, and she responded to their applause with an encore. Through these meetings, Betty got to know many of the wives of lawyers for utilities from throughout the country (separate activities were always scheduled for the wives), several of whom also ultimately became wives of utility CEOs.

Betty and Jack had intermittent contacts with activities at Yale throughout this period. Although other Wiggin & Dana partners were the firm's primary contacts with the university, during the period of the Black Panther riots in New Haven, President Kingman Brewster asked Jack's advice as to Yale's appropriate actions. Brewster also asked Jack to act as mediator of a dispute with a female doctoral candidate who had been denied her degree and one with a faculty member in the Chinese language school who had been terminated. On several occasions, Jack complied with requests from Professor Brown at the Law School to participate in seminars in his courses, and on a few occasions, when a judge scheduled to preside at an evening session of Moot Court (a mandatory activity for first-year law students) cancelled unexpectedly, Jack was asked to pinch-hit since he was available on short notice. It was at one of those sessions that Jack first met Joy's former Wellesley tower-mate, when he was a substitute judge on the night of her argument and joined the informal critique session that followed the arguments. Betty and Jack subsequently met both of the Clintons during Jack's term as a member of the Law School Alumni Board. They attended a dinner where Bill was the featured speaker and he spoke at great length about his education program for Arkansas, but he had not yet sharpened his oratorical skills, which resulted in many in the audience nodding. Betty always assumed these two Law School events accounted for she and Jack receiving a Christmas card from the Clintons each year they occupied the White House since Jack had no other affiliation with them or with the Democratic Party.

In an attempt to balance his business and litigation practices during this period, Jack played a major role in expanding Wiggin & Dana by hiring a number of new associates. One associate, who became one of the firm's primary litigators, was a young lawyer who had practiced for several years at a large Wall Street firm and sought a less urban practice. He was referred to Jack by one of Justice Clark's 1953-term clerks who had become a partner in that Wall Street firm. Jack also interviewed and Wiggin & Dana hired Joe Lieberman when he graduated from Yale Law School in 1967. Joe worked on litigation with Jack for a couple of years, but he then decided he preferred politics. Betty always entertained the new associates and their wives and enjoyed that function.

While Joy had been happy with her experience at North Haven High School, Betty and Jack decided, after discussing the matter with advisors at the high school, that the scientific education offered there was limited. Accordingly, rather than following his sister to the local school, son Jack, commencing in 1965, became a student at Taft School in Watertown, Connecticut, which not only had a challenging science curriculum, but already was offering learning opportunities with respect to the emerging field of computers. Jack quickly acclimated to being a boarding student at Taft and, despite admonitions to avoid contact sports due to his eye, went out for, and enjoyed playing on, the prep school soccer team. During his years at Taft, Betty made many journeys to regional prep schools, including as far afield as Deerfield, Massachusetts, to cheer for the Taft soccer team.

Having missed a summer trip in 1963 and having had only a couple of weeks at a rental cottage on the shore in Ocean City, Maryland, in 1964, the Fassetts decided to resume their more challenging vacation routines in 1965 by renting a small, new house trailer and camping on Cape Hatteras. The trailer was a concession to two-year-old Lora and her aging parents, but young Jack and Joy, and a high-school classmate who accompanied her, still slept in tents. The group had a wonderful time with sunny weather at a virtually deserted campground at Frisco. They did a lot of swimming, fishing, crabbing, and exploring, being interrupted only when a state police officer located Jack to deliver the message that he was wanted back in Hartford sooner than planned since a federal judge had scheduled a special summer hearing in the reapportionment case. Despite this development, on the rescheduled return trip, the vacationers were able to visit Jamestown, Williamsburg, and Yorktown, Virginia. The return trip was made even more exciting when a wheel came off the trailer on a highway in Maryland, resulting in the vacationers having a couple more days at the beach in Ocean City (accommodated by the Fassetts' landlady of the previous year) while a new axle was procured by a garage to repair the trailer.

During Joy's junior year in high school, where she had been active in singing groups and as a member of the debating team, Betty and Jack undertook to take her on a tour of possible colleges (including Cornell University, where her beau had been admitted to a special program for talented youngsters promising both undergraduate and doctoral degrees in five years). Over one winter weekend, they visited Bryn Mawr and Swarthmore in Pennsylvania and a frigid Cornell in Ithaca, New York. On a subsequent weekend, they toured Radcliffe and Wellesley colleges in the Boston area, and Joy ultimately adopted her parents' first choice. She applied for early admission to, and, as a National Merit Scholar, was accepted by, Wellesley College in Wellesley, Massachusetts. A dramatic coincidence of that choice was that when, during her freshman year, Joy brought her dormitory roommate with her for a weekend visit to North Haven, Betty discovered that Susan was the daughter of Chaplain Andrews, who had served with Betty in Europe in the 134th Evacuation Hospital.

During 1966, Betty, Jack, and children made a number of trips to the World's Fair in Flushing Meadows, New York, where the 1939–1940 Fair had also been held. The following year, with the family nest emptying with Joy as well as Jack away at schools, Betty and Jack decided to change the format as well as the timing of their annual vacations. In 1967, for the first time, they took a weeklong winter vacation to Bermuda, staying at Deepdene Manor in mid-island. With Lora, they swam, explored the entire island, and enjoyed eating grapefruit from trees in the yard at the inn.

While Lora was still preschool, Jack was attending Taft, and Joy had just completed her first year at Wellesley, Betty joined in planning what proved to be the last family camping vacation. In late June 1968, the family (without equipment since a large tent and other equipment were available for rental at the site) flew to St. Thomas in the American Virgin Islands. After purchasing a couple of weeks' supply of groceries there, they took a small passenger ferry to the island of St. John, which contained little except the ritzy Rockefeller Caneel Bay Resort and a national park with a spacious campground on the fabulous beach on Cinnamon Bay. Both Joy and Jack soon joined their father in becoming eager snorkelers, but Betty never could be convinced to keep her face submerged underwater long enough to learn to snorkel. In a rented Jeep, the Fassetts toured the largely uninhabited island of abandoned sugar plantations until it was time to take a seaplane trip (boarded from a rowboat) from St. John to St. Croix. On that more-developed island, they stayed a motel called the Pink Fancy (reportedly once a bordello), swam in the pool and at the National Underwater Park, and the parents were introduced by a vacationing Air Force colonel and his wife to the variety of drinks that could be concocted in a blender from local rum and a variety of local fruits.

During 1969, Betty and Jack had two traveling adventures, only one of which was entirely a vacation. First, once again trusting Lora to a neighbor, the Fassetts took a direct flight from New York to Montego Bay on the island of Jamaica, where they had reserved a four-wheel-drive vehicle. Driving British-style for the first time (the opposite lane from in the states), Jack drove along the coastal road to the resort town of Ocho Rios. Staying in a waterfront hotel, the Fassetts had a great time sunning on the pretty beach, observing the peacocks that congregated outside their lodging, going into town to view the natives and their crafts, and overeating. In addition, Jack experienced one of the greatest scares of his life. Since Betty did not snorkel, each day Jack would snorkel alone out to, and along, the fabulous coral reef which was a considerable distance out from the sandy beach. One day, while admiring the beautiful fish along the reef, Jack spotted a huge shark foraging nearby. Violating all snorkeling rules, Jack turned and headed for shore as fast as his flippers would allow him to swim. Having escaped that time, Jack never thereafter snorkeled alone and for a long time afterward he periodically would have a nightmare about the experience.

Having seen the touristy portion of Jamaica, Betty and Jack decided also to visit other aspects of the country. Accordingly, they took a short ride up the coast to view a large aluminum smelting plant and its busy harbor facilities and, contrary to advice given at their hotel, undertook a drive on the narrow road over the mountains to the capital city of Kingston. There they visited the university and some government buildings, but also some of the worst slums they had ever observed, with raw sewage running in the gutters along alleys of overpopulated shacks.

A meeting of the EEI Legal Committee was scheduled for the Broadmoor Hotel outside Colorado Springs, Colorado, in mid-October 1969. The president of UI asked Jack to expand his trip to attend a meeting in Denver involving financial matters concerning utilities, so Betty and Jack planned to do a little sightseeing in that part of Colorado before going to the Broadmoor. When the Fassetts' flight arrived in Denver, an early-season blizzard was in progress and snow was still falling as they departed in their rental car into the Rockies and past the ski resort at Vail to Grand Junction. Since it was also snowing there, they headed south through the San Juan and Gunnison national forests, above the majestic Black Canyon of the Gunnison, and through old mining towns to Durango. They spent one night at a small inn in the mountains where they were served fresh-caught mountain trout that was sautéed and filleted by the chef next to their dining table. At Durango, they detoured westward a short distance to visit Mesa Verde National Park and to climb the trails and ladders to its amazing cliff dwellings. Since snow was again threatening and they still had a few days before Jack's meeting, they again headed south and visited Santa Fe, New Mexico, before terminating their detour in Albuquerque. Baseball's World Series was in progress, so they watched one game in their Albuquerque motel before hastening back north over snowy terrain to the Broadmoor with only a brief stop in arty Taos. As a result of the early snow, the road up Pikes Peak was already closed for the season, but on their return trip to the Denver airport, they were able to drive around the impressive facilities (and visit the large, A-frame chapel) of the Air Force Academy in Colorado Springs.

Joy's engagement to Paul Mermin, her beau since high school, was announced in the *New Haven Register* in late 1969. Thereafter, Betty, recovering from an extended hospitalization at Yale–New Haven for a hysterectomy performed by Dr. Billings, set to work with her sewing machine, the use of which she had mastered in recent years, making Joy's wedding gown and the gowns for Joy's bridesmaids as well as a dress for Lora. The interfaith wedding was held in December 1970 in the chapel at Yale, and the reception, attended by Betty and Jack's many friends and many of his legal and business associates, Paul's family, and Joy and Paul's cohorts from their rebellious anti–Vietnam War generation, was held at the Quinnipiack Club, an old downtown New Haven club where Jack generally ate his lunch when in the city and where Betty liked to dine in the evening on special occasions. Joy, having been elected to Phi Beta Kappa, graduated from Wellesley during an impressive ceremony on June 5, 1971. On that day, Betty was reunited for the first time with Chaplain Andrews, Susan's father, by then a national leader of his church.

Earlier that year, growing more adventurous again, when Lora had her spring vacation from first grade at Ridge Road School (another school realignment), Betty, Jack, and Lora booked a two-week visit at a remote retreat Betty had seen advertised in a small ad in *The New York Times*. Flying by jet plane to Barbados, they transferred to a four-seater plane for the short flight to Nevis, where they landed in a field that first had to be cleared of grazing goats. They spent an intriguing two weeks in a cottage on the side of the volcanic mountain that made up the island, enjoying, during most of their stay, being the only guests at Golden Rock Estate (one of the many former sugar plantations in the Caribbean). Nevis was famous mostly as the birthplace of Alexander Hamilton and the favorite spot of Lord Hamilton (not related to Alexander) when he was admiral of England's Caribbean fleet. Each day when the American-born operator of the inn asked Jack what she should purchase for that night's dinner on her daily trip to the local market, he replied "lobster," so the Fassetts consumed many of the Caribbean crustaceans, which are quite different than those from Maine. The Fassetts mostly swam in the rain-filled swimming pool in front of their cottage, but one day their hostess offered her car and its native driver to take them to swim at the small sandy ocean beach and to see the town and the natural hot baths. On another day, the driver took them on a tour of the parts of the small island they had not seen.

Golden Rock had a single somewhat-rough tennis court, and the hostess provided Betty and Jack with racquets and well-worn balls so they could play. Betty enjoyed that return to her old-favorite sport and, upon returning home, the family became members of the New Haven Lawn Club, an old New Haven organization that had a large clubhouse with a spacious ballroom, a good dining room, four squash courts, locker and shower rooms for both sexes, and eight red-clay tennis courts supervised by an able pro, Lois Felix, who had once won a doubles title at Wimbledon. Betty promptly became deeply involved in regular games at the club and shortly became a member of the club's women's team, which played matches with teams from other clubs. For many years thereafter, it became a ritual for the Fassetts to join a group of new tennis friends each Saturday for lunch (Jack still did office work on Saturday mornings) and for an afternoon of tennis matches. Betty played doubles with the ladies while Jack engaged in endless sets of singles with Keith Zimmermann, Andy Wong (head of ophthalmology at Yale), and several other equally ardent competitors. Lora took some lessons from Lois Felix and became a good player. She and her father won the parent-child club tournament one year and, occasionally, Betty and Jack would engage in mixed doubles contests with Keith and Mary Jane or Andy and Irene.

Having enjoyed their recent ventures beyond the border of the country to remote islands, Betty, Jack, and Lora, during spring breaks in succeeding years while Lora attended the new Green Acres School built by the town a few blocks north of Bishop Street, traveled to two remote islands in the Bahamas chain. Going to Exuma, they had stops with brief stays each way at a hotel in Nassau, but Eastern Airlines had a direct flight to Eleuthera, reportedly since its president had a home there. At the Out-Island Inn on Exuma, Jack enjoyed good snorkeling, but Betty and Lora preferred the family's expeditions around the island on rented bicycles. On Eleuthera, there were tennis courts, so that sport was the favorite pastime along with hiking and eating.

Upon each return, Jack resumed his expanding responsibilities for UI, including as its representative on the Executive Committee of the New England Power Pool, which involved monthly two-day trips to Westboro, Massachusetts. He had earlier made similar trips while a member of the working committee that had developed the historic NEPOOL Agreement and had also represented his client in negotiating agreements regarding ownership of interests in jointly owned nuclear power plants planned for construction in Connecticut, Massachusetts, and New Hampshire.

With son Jack now busy specializing in science courses at Brown University in Providence, Rhode Island, and Joy married and pursuing her teaching career at a school in Middlefield, Connecticut (she had taught at Ridge Road School in North Haven her first year, thus creating the anomaly of a teacher and a beginning student being sisters), where she had gone to participate in an innovative teaching program, during their 1972 island vacation, Betty, Jack and Lora traveled with Rusty and Bob Hart. Due to an airline strike, they were routed from New York to Toronto, Canada, where they boarded a direct flight to Barbados. After a tour of English Harbor, Sam Lord's Castle, and other sights on that very civilized island, they took a small plane to their destination, Grand Anse Beach Inn on the "spice island" of Grenada, the largest of the Grenadine Islands. It was a most enjoyable sojourn and, despite his breathing handicap, Bob became an ardent snorkeler in Jack's company. The group drove to the "nutmeg factory" in their rented Jeep and, while it was long prior to the days of the American invasion of the island, political unrest was rife and the tourist group beat a hasty retreat during their venture when, while stopped to eat their lunches, they were approached by a quartet of men wielding machetes.

The major event of 1972 for the Fassetts was their moving to a new home, acquired early in the spring. For several years, Betty and Jack had been observing transactions in the real estate market in a small part of North Haven closer to the city called Old Orchard (the area once had been a large apple orchard adjacent to the mansion owned by A. C. Gilbert, famed for inventing and manufacturing erector sets, chemistry kits, and other educational toys). Early in the year, Jack made an offer, which was accepted, for a large, brick and stone, ranch-style house on a large lot on the corner of Old Orchard Road and Skiff Street. The location reminded Betty of Seneca Parkway since the road had a center island planted with dogwood trees that flowered profusely each spring. One of Jack's older partners had once resided on the street, and four of the Fassett's nearest neighbors were doctor-acquaintances of Betty and Jack. Betty, somewhat reluctantly, left the Bishop Street property on which she had spent so much time and energy, but she liked the new yard and the house with its large living room and stone fireplace, the huge family room with another fireplace on the lower level, the bigger kitchen, and the large two-car garage attached to the house in its rear by another smaller recreation room. Since Betty had had her own car for a number of years, the garage, which was entered from a driveway from Skiff Street, was most welcome in snowy North Haven. Jack again had a curved front driveway and an oak-paneled den that easily housed his desk, books, and other den furniture. The transaction was facilitated by the fact that the agent who sold the Old Orchard home also quickly produced a purchaser for the Bishop Street property which, with all of the Fassetts' enhancements, sold for several times its original cost.

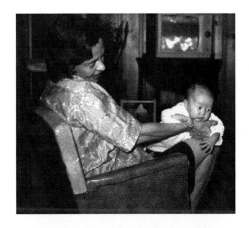

Baby Lora joins the clan, 1963

Vacationing with baby and trailer, Cape Hatteras, 1965

New York World's Fair, 1966

Betty and Chaplain Andrews
at Wellesley

Sophomore Father's Day. 1969

Joy and Paul's
wedding,
1970

"Town Fathers" and wives, North Haven Policemen's Ball

*Matching nightshirts
Christmas, 1972*

～12～

Old Orchard Road, 1972–1978

Within a few months of moving to her new home, which she liked, Betty began to learn why the prior owners had been such eager sellers. The first New Year's Eve, since she and Jack were partying with their usual group and Lora was visiting a friend, she gave Joy and Jack permission to invite their friends to their new home for a party. The partyers had a good time, but before the New Year was very old, the bathroom adjoining the family room began to back up and overflow. A few days later, with lots of snow on the ground, a heavy rainfall occurred and, despite the fact that the Fassetts' property was on the top of a ridge, water seeped into the basement until it was six inches deep and the wiring to the baseboard electric heating in the family room was shorting. Since Jack was in Westboro, Betty called his office for assistance. The financial vice president wisely advised Betty to stay away from the water, and within an hour a UI crew had the problem under temporary control. A contractor they recommended promptly replaced the sewer line, which had become clogged by the roots of a large willow tree that adorned the Skiff Street side of the house, and installed new pipes and two sump pumps to deal with the flooding. With those problems resolved, Betty decided that the family room should have pine paneling like at Bishop Street (Betty loved wooden walls and furniture; she had spent many hours sanding and waxing a solid-cherry farm table given to her, and it still adorns the entry hall in Joy's Chapel Hill home), so Jack undertook that project. However, when she decided a darker-wood wall would be nice in the large living room, the carpenters who had built the Bishop Street addition were summoned and they installed an eye-catching wall of solid walnut from the material she selected.

Not only the interior of the Old Orchard Road house soon underwent changes from Betty's efforts and supervision. Desiring not to have so much grass, Betty began planting pachysandra in two areas on the Skiff Street side and front during the first spring, and those beds continued to expand for the next couple of years. A doctor neighbor, having frequently seen Betty kneeling and planting shoots she had obtained from

Sela Barker's large source on Ridge Road, dubbed Betty "the pachysandra queen" and the name stuck for a while. All of the neighbors were active people: across the street were the families of the owner of the largest department store in New Haven and of a doctor who had a private practice, but also was retained by UI as its medical director; the two next-door neighbors were a businessman who was on the UI board and his wife and the widow of the former president of New Haven Savings Bank. There was considerable socializing among all of the residents of the road. Most of the yards (including Fassetts' rear) still contained old apple trees from the orchard days and, each year in the fall, two of the doctors would rent a cider press and the whole neighborhood would enjoy fresh cider and a cookout. Betty supervised Jack's installation of a split rail fence around their property and the construction by a carpenter of a new wooden deck off the living room in the rear. The yard already contained a variety of trees to which were added a Japanese cherry and two red maples not far from the front and rear picture windows of the living room. Betty frequently stated that she did not have to go to Vermont in the fall to see the foliage because her yard was even more dramatic. She loved to watch the proliferation of birds (and squirrels), especially the cardinals, that fed at her several feeders.

During their first year of residence on Old Orchard Road there were many pivotal changes in the lives of the Fassetts. Shortly after completing the move, Betty and Lora flew to Pittsburgh, where her parents had moved after Dutch's retirement from the railroad. While they were away, in early June, Jack made an excursion to an important NEPOOL meeting in Westboro with UI's CEO. At the time, there was a vacancy on the federal Court of Appeals covering Connecticut, New York, and Vermont, about which there had been much speculation in the media as to who would be appointed to the judgeship by President Nixon. During a break in the NEPOOL meeting, a representative from another utility congratulated Jack on his possible appointment to the position. When UI's startled CEO questioned the action, an article from the prior day's *Hartford Courant* was produced indicating that Jack was a strong candidate, though not backed by Connecticut's Senator Lowell Weicker. While Jack had been aware that his candidacy had been proposed by a bar group and endorsed by a number of federal court judges, whose annual meetings he had been invited to for a number of years as a representative of the Connecticut trial bar, he had not been forewarned about the *Courant* article and had not considered his appointment to be a likely occurrence since the backing of senators is traditionally the key to such appointments. (President Nixon shortly resolved his problem by appointing a judge from New York, despite the fact that it theoretically was Connecticut's turn for an appointment.) The disclosure, indicating a possibility that Jack would leave Wiggin & Dana, resulted in UI's CEO importuning Jack on their return trip to New Haven to make a firm commitment not to accept any judgeship and to accept a position as number two in command at UI, with the titles of vice president and general counsel. Since a prompt response was requested, Betty's concurrence in Jack's decision, once again to make a fundamental career change, was given during a long telephone conversation between North Haven and Pittsburgh.

After a rapid convivial resolution of Jack's partnership interest in Wiggin & Dana and transfer of his litigation responsibilities for all of his pending cases to other lawyers in the firm, Jack and his law library moved across the New Haven Green and a little over four blocks to the headquarters of UI at 80 Temple

Street. A new office and adjoining space for Jack's legal secretary, who opted to follow him to the new location, had been refurbished on the opposite side of the boardroom from the CEO's.

Since he had been so heavily involved in UI's affairs for a number of years, Jack quickly felt comfortable in his new position. During the next spring, Jack took a short vacation and, with Lora on break from Ridge Road School, to which she had transferred as a consequence of the Old Orchard move, the Fassetts flew to Grand Cayman Island in the Cayman Group. There they swam (the snorkeling was poor) and visited the large turtle farm and butchery for which the island was known. Betty's primary memories of that trip are of having caught a large bonefish while fishing and of having eaten goat stew in a native eatery while live goats wandered the premises. After finishing at Ridge Road and a few terms riding the school bus to the town's junior high school, together with the daughter of an Old Orchard neighbor, Lora began attending Choate–Rosemary Hall in Wallingford, Connecticut, as a day student. After a few terms of riding in a carpool, in which Betty was one of the drivers, and thus missing many of the prep school's extracurricular activities, Lora enthusiastically opted to become a boarding student for her final years at Choate.

Betty and Jack attended son Jack's graduation at Brown University on June 4, 1973, where he received a bachelor's degree in science, honors in chemistry, and award of a fellowship to Cornell to pursue his doctorate in that field. After having celebrated their fiftieth anniversary earlier that year (Betty's parents had celebrated theirs in 1969), Jack's parents in 1973 enjoyed a Christmas with their grandchildren for the first time on Old Orchard Road. Shortly after being driven back to Stamford at the end of the holidays, Jack's father collapsed and died, adding grief to the tumultuous events that unfolded during the end of that year with the commencement of the Yom Kippur War and the ensuing Arab oil embargo. While there were shortages of gasoline throughout the nation, the embargo created a crisis for the electric utility industry, especially in New England, whose utilities, including UI, were heavily dependent on imported oil to operate their generating plants.

As a result of the oil crisis, Jack not only spent many days in Massachusetts at NEPOOL working with representatives of other utilities trying to ensure that at least a livable level of electricity would keep flowing in New England, but also many hours at public hearings called in response to increasing electric rates and with politicians and political aspirants who took advantage of the crisis to attack both the state utility regulators and the assertedly greedy utility executives. Betty was not immune from this situation. Since Jack refused to have a private telephone line at his office or an unlisted number at their home (a policy he continued throughout his tenure at UI), Betty fielded a number of calls from irate UI customers and even a few confrontations, some from tennis players at the Lawn Club. She received even more calls, primarily from acquaintances residing in New Haven's suburbs where lots of trees mingled with power lines, when, during Jack's first year at UI, southern Connecticut suffered a devastating ice storm that took down many electric lines, causing widespread outages. Shortly after moving onto Old Orchard Road, the Fassetts had purchased a wood-burning Franklin stove for the large basement family room and, during several of the crises, Betty shut off the electric heat in the main portion of the house and cooked and served dinner on the Franklin stove. When she would hear a complaint about high electric bills, she would diplomatically advise the complainer of ways to conserve energy and cite the reduction she had accomplished in the Fassetts' usage. When an eager UI supervisor stopped at her home during one of the outages that encompassed Old Orchard Road and offered to expedite the restoration of service, she declined having her house restored until the entire neighborhood had electric service again.

Facing the turmoil in the industry, UI's CEO decided, in less than a year after Jack joined the company, to begin his retirement. The directors asked Jack to assume the reins as of September 1, 1974, so Betty unexpectedly became not only the wife of a utility executive, but the wife of one of the industry's beleaguered CEOs. She enthusiastically fulfilled that role for over ten busy years. Since one aspect of the change in command involved the retiring CEO becoming chairman of the board, Jack was assigned the duty of advising the existing chairman, who had formerly been CEO and had retired to Longboat Key in Florida. Betty, Jack, and Lora flew to Sarasota, where they were picked up and entertained royally for several days by that chairman and his wife. Jack broke the news to him about the board's decision as the group strolled the lovely beach of the Key, which unfortunately was then littered with dead fish because of an incident of red tide.

Betty encouraged Jack in his determination to change the staid image the electric industry had historically achieved. As soon as all of the major improvements had been completed, all of the directors and officers of UI and their wives were invited to a cocktail and dinner party so that many of them could meet for the first time. It was a grand success and became an annual UI ritual, although the site was subsequently changed to the Lawn Club where there was more room for toasts, humorous awards, and sometimes entertainment. One year a Yale singing group performed, and another year a talented couple sang duets. UI and its industry were completely dominated by white males when Jack became CEO. His first steps within his first year were to promote a longtime female employee, who had done some good work for the Public Relations Department (renamed the Communications Department in the first reorganization), to be assistant vice president of the renamed department and an able, young black man in the Engineering Department to be assistant vice president for environmental engineering. He also created a new position in the Personnel Department for diversity advancement and training. Jack also obtained the board's approval to add a female to that body (one of Jack's law school contemporaries, then on the Yale faculty, happily accepted his offer of the board position and served very effectively for a few years until the governor appointed her to the state supreme court, of which she ultimately became chief justice). These changes were well received by the company's employees and Jack's fellow officers and were soon matched by a wave of similar actions throughout the industry.

The Old Orchard house was a good location for parties, and although Betty generally was not enthusiastic about large parties, in January 1976 she succeeded in arranging an affair that was a complete surprise to Jack to celebrate his fiftieth birthday. With Jack relaxed and ready to spend a quiet evening, all of the Fassetts' usual New Year's Eve crowd plus several of their tennis-playing friends, a couple of Jack's former law partners, and Jack's predecessor as CEO at UI and his wife arrived with several carrying prepared dishes and many presenting humorous items such as a shopping basket with fifty oranges and the bottle of Geritol that had been circulating for many years (and was then finally retired). As the bicentennial of the nation's founding, 1976 was also celebrated by the congregating in New York City, from all over the world, of the tall ships. Not only old sailing vessels arrived, but also many modern ships and, with wharfing space scarce, Jack agreed to allow a Swedish naval vessel to moor at the dock (constructed to accommodate oil tankers) at UI's recently completed power plant on New Haven harbor for the week of the festivities. One evening, Betty and Jack and a few other UI executives and their wives were hosted on board the vessel for a cocktail party and a dinner of typical Swedish naval fare, which made Betty happy that she had not spent her military career in the Swedish navy. The captain presented Jack with a replica of an ancient naval cannon, which still reposes among his treasures.

During this period, Mary Jane Zimmermann asked Betty to join her in a group whose function was to welcome to the New Haven community exchange students from foreign countries. In 1977, Betty became sponsor for a Japanese economics professor who came to Yale for a year and brought his wife and two young daughters. Betty became deeply involved in their lives, finding a house for them to rent in Hamden; enrolling the girls in the public school, where they proved to be excellent students; and even helping the professor purchase a used car. The couple entertained the Fassetts in their home with a typical Japanese meal and, when the family returned to Wesleyan College in Middletown, Connecticut, several years later, the professor brought his family to North Haven to renew their friendship. When the professor indicated an interest in the fact that Betty sang in her church choir, she brought him along to a practice and, having a good voice, he became a choir member for the balance of their Yale visit.

The Fassetts enjoyed many visitors to their Old Orchard Road home. Of particular note, Betty's father drove himself and her mother to see the new home, and Dutch and Jack had a good time playing pool on the pool table that had been added to a room off the basement family room. Chick and Ray Rapp visited from California, and Betty guided them on tours of Yale and other New Haven sights.

With all of the problems facing UI and all of his other commitments, Jack was unable to schedule a trip to another Caribbean island until 1978. Then, once again with Rusty and Bob Hart, and with Lora along, the Fassetts flew to Trinidad and from there to the island of Tobago for a restful week. The cottage on Tobago was on a high cliff overlooking the sea, yet neither the beach, the snorkeling, nor the island itself were near as pleasant or interesting as Grenada had been.

During a bridge session with the Harts on a Wednesday night preceding a Labor Day weekend in the mid-1970s, while Lora was still on vacation from her school, Bob stated that he sure would like to be on the island of Nantucket for the holiday weekend. One of his longtime patients had recently moved there to operate a boardinghouse. When Rusty and Betty enthusiastically concurred and Jack said he would provide the transportation if Bob could provide the rooms, Bob made a late-night call to his surprised patient who was happy to offer rooms since many of the college students who boarded at her facility while performing summer jobs on the island already had departed. Shortly after dawn on the following Saturday, Betty, Rusty, Lora, Bob, and Jack boarded a six-seater twin-engine aircraft at New Haven Airport and in just over an hour landed at Nantucket Airport to be greeted by Bob's benefactor who loaned the group her car to be used for the weekend. A fine time was had swimming, fishing, clamming, eating, and sightseeing until the plane returned on Monday for the trip back to New Haven. As on the trip out, loading of the plane was a challenge since Bob's and Jack's surf-casting rods could only be conveyed by carrying them in the cabin, which required considerable bending of them.

For several years following the Labor Day excursion, the Fassetts, through Bob's friend, rented a cottage for several weeks or a month each summer above the dunes at Smith Point, which was several miles from the town in Nantucket (the Harts were Smith Point neighbors one of those years). By then, Joy and Paul had moved to Middlefield where Joy was teaching in elementary school and Paul was working toward his master's degree in psychology at Wesleyan University. They were able to join the assemblage at the summer cottage, but son Jack and his wife were still busy in Ithaca and not able to get to the island. Miriam Bolotin, a classmate of Jack's at Brown, had also gone to Cornell for graduate studies, and they had been married in 1976 in Ithaca with a wedding party at their new apartment in an old Ithaca mansion. Betty's father had died suddenly in 1975, and, one subsequent year, Betty's mother and Jack's mother both joined the group at the Nantucket cottage. Betty and Jack marveled at the pair of widows walking arm-in-arm down the beach and down the street in the town.

Most years, after arriving on the island from the long ferry ride, Betty and Lora would stay at the cottage for the whole rental period. Since Jack had frequent nonpostponable hearings to attend for company interests (hearings with regulators with respect to financings and electric rates and meetings of NEPOOL and of the joint owners of the Seabrook project), he usually was flown in and out of Nantucket for visits of a weekend or a few days. While there, Jack always went clamming, at the sound side of Smith Point, in the early morning, and the cottage's refrigerator was always filled with containers of freshly dug clams which made a hissing noise when its door was opened. Every evening after dinner, Jack would surf-cast for bluefish, and occasionally he would also catch a large striped bass. Betty's daily routine, upon getting all in residence fed in the morning, was to take a container of the large quahogs from the refrigerator, along with her more manageable shorter fishing rod, and spend her time until noon on a breakwater on the sound side fishing for flounder or whatever else chose to take her bait. Occasionally she would hook a large eel and have to seek help from some other willing fisherman to remove the critter from her hook. The balance of the quahogs, not used for bait, were used to feed the pot of clam chowder that was constantly residing on the stove. All of the cherrystone clams were eagerly consumed on the half-shell in the evenings as hors d'oeuvres. Betty enjoyed participating in the endless SCRABBLE games and other games constantly being played in the cottage. One year, the group undertook to make a large hooked rug on the big, heavy, wooden table that was the centerpiece of the great room at the cottage. The rug was completed by Betty following the vacation and was in front of a fireplace at Old Orchard Road for some years.

Old Orchard Road

ABOVE LEFT: *Lora with dogwoods, in the island of Old Orchard Road*
ABOVE RIGHT: *Christmas, 1977, Jack, Joy Paul, Mimi*
LOWER RIGHT: *Jack and Betty relaxing on the back porch*

With international friends from Japan, the Shibuyis:
AT LEFT: *In church*
ABOVE: *Thanksgiving*

*Chick and Ray Rapp visit and tour
the Yale campus with Jack and Betty*

*Vacationing on Tobago with Bob
and Rusty Hart, 1978*

Summer on Nantucket – cooking and fishing

*Jack's 50th
birthday party*

*Jack and Mimi's
wedding*

ᐸ13ᐳ

OLD ORCHARD ROAD, 1979–1982

The waning of the first oil crisis was soon succeeded for the utilities of New England by new crises regarding obtaining licenses—despite public protests and political opposition—for nuclear plants planned to reduce the region's heavy dependence on imported oil, and regarding obtaining financing to construct the expensive units. Because of Jack's involvement in these matters, particularly with respect to the Seabrook Station in New Hampshire (UI was co–lead owner with Public Service of New Hampshire of the Seabrook plant at the outset, but, when the crisis deepened and PSNH got in financial trouble, Jack had to assume control of the massive project for all of the joint owners), Betty became directly involved by becoming his chauffeur to meetings so he could work en route. With Boston meetings, Betty would shop (she liked Filene's Basement) or sightsee; on Seabrook trips, she would spend time at the visitor center or, on occasion, be given a tour of the construction site. When Jack, in 1979, became president of the Electric Council of New England, the regional trade association, Betty joined him for all of the annual and midyear meetings during his two-year term. It was not a great burden since the winter meetings were held at such resorts as Chatham on Cape Cod and Prout's Neck in Maine and the summer meetings at such Vermont sites as Stratford Mountain and Woodstock, thus enjoying great sites at off-season rates. The Council operated a two-week school each summer at a resort facility in Vermont where each member could send a quota of middle-management employees for intensive schooling on utility matters. The classes were taught by other personnel from the companies and by hired outside experts. Betty spent several days at two such sessions during which Jack did some lecturing. She became acquainted with UI's contingent, several of whom went on to high positions, and all of them always thereafter inquired about her.

The wife of an active utility CEO had to become proficient at attending all kinds of meetings. The top priority was industry gatherings, and since Jack was elected as one of the Northeast representatives on the

Board of Edison Electric Institute shortly after he became president of UI, Betty got to meet a lot more of the industry's top people and visit some different resorts than had occurred during Jack's tenure on the legal committee. One year the board met at the Camelback Inn in Scottsdale, Arizona, and the president of Iowa Electric, who chose to stay at John Gardner's famous tennis resort in the same city, invited the Fassetts to come to his cottage during a break in the meetings and play some tennis. When the EEI meetings were held in Boston and Philadelphia, interesting sites, such as the Boston Atheneum and a historic colonial meeting hall, were made available for meetings.

Most utility CEOs were golfers, but there was a contingent of tennis-playing executives so there was some competitive tennis at meeting places. When an industry group one year met in Palm Springs, California, EBASCO sponsored a serious tennis tournament among the attendees, and Jack was awarded a large silver trophy at the final dinner. After a few years, that award disappeared from Jack's den because Betty got tired of polishing it. The year the EEI board met at Pebble Beach, also in California, Betty and Jack flew into San Francisco and spent a couple of nights at the home of Chick and Ray Rapp in Berkeley, where their old friends had settled and Ray had a thriving surgical practice. The Fassetts' journeys for EEI board meetings culminated in 1981 when that smaller group was entertained by the local utility CEO in his antebellum home in suburban New Orleans while the larger annual meeting of EEI met in the large arena downtown in that picturesque city. Following the final meeting, the Fassetts, joined by the Luces (Charlie was CEO of Consolidated Edison in New York City) and the Carlsons (Ted was CEO of Central Hudson Electric) rushed to the airport to catch an Eastern Airlines evening flight to New York. As the Boeing 727 approached its destination, the pilot announced that there was a problem with the landing gear, a fact Betty had already detected when she did not hear the wheels descend. After the plane detoured over the ocean to dump fuel, all of the passenger were told to empty their pockets of sharp objects and to assume a fetallike position, the lights were extinguished, and the plane crash-landed and skidded off the runway. It was quickly surrounded by ambulances and fire trucks as all of the passengers and crew hastily exited by chute or over the wing. Fortunately, there were no serious injuries. The article accompanying a photo of the crash on the front page of one of the next morning's New York papers proclaimed "72 safe in JFK crash-landing" and quoted Jack as saying "of the ordeal": "I've had a lot of worse landings with the wheels down."

Since Jack was chairman of the Greater New Haven Chamber of Commerce from 1979 to 1981 and its annual membership dinner meeting at a downtown New Haven hotel was scheduled shortly after the crash, Jack told the large audience of Betty's and his adventure during his good-bye speech during which he introduced that year's guest speaker, Senator William Proxmire, then much publicized for his efforts at the apparently impossible task of eliminating wasteful spending by the federal government. Three years earlier, when Jack was vice chairman, Betty had also sat on the dais as Jack's predecessor had introduced CIA Director George Bush, who was happy to accept an invitation to return to Connecticut where he still had many relatives and where the Bush's first son was born. Betty compared some recollections about living on Hillhouse Avenue with him. Since Jack had also rashly accepted the position of chairman of the Connecticut Public Expenditure Council, the taxpayer association supported primarily by businesses and industry to monitor budgets and spending by the state, during the same two-year period as he chaired the chamber, Betty had many opportunities to sit at the dais and to hostess meetings from 1979 to 1981.

To Betty's dismay, Jack having convinced her a few years after he became CEO that his accepting a directorship at Barnes Group—a large manufacturing company headquartered in Bristol, Connecticut, and headed by one of Jack's classmates from his original law school class—would result in some interesting trips, the only trips she received were to annual meetings in Connecticut. No wives were invited on the two board meetings that were held in cities in Mexico and Brazil where the manufacturer of various kinds of springs had manufacturing facilities.

In 1979, having given up on having any long vacations, Betty and Jack took a quick trip to Florida and, after checking several possible locations, signed a contract to purchase a condominium scheduled to be constructed in an island community on the Gulf side of St. Petersburg called Isla del Sol. A major attribute of the location was its fast access from Tampa Airport (located where Drew Field Hospital, Betty's first army assignment had been located during WWII), to which there were frequent flights from either New York or Hartford airports by several airlines. Arrangements were made for the unit to be furnished since Betty had insufficient time to do any furniture shopping. After completion of the unit, which faced a long fairway on the island's golf course and had a large pool and spa, during the last years of Jack's full-time employment at UI, instead of Nantucket, Betty and Jack snuck short periods at Isla. When the Choate girls' tennis team, of which Lora was captain, with their coach, came in a school van to the University of South Florida in Tampa during their spring break the year after the condo was completed for early tennis practice, the whole group used the Isla condo, most sleeping in sleeping bags on the floor, to extend their sojourn. Betty and Jack also loaned use of the unit a couple of times including, on one occasion, to Jack's faithful secretary and her UI receptionist friend for their summer vacation.

In anticipation of Lora's graduation from Choate, her parents took her on a college exploration tour, but, unlike her older sister, she was not interested in staying in the East and preferred the South. After seriously considering the University of North Carolina in Chapel Hill and Emory University in Atlanta, Lora chose to enter Duke University in Durham, North Carolina, in the fall of 1981. Initially, she planned to pursue a program that promised degrees in both nursing and science, but she changed her mind about nursing as a career and did not pursue a degree in any medical field until she was in graduate school. By the time Lora had matriculated at Duke, Joy and Paul had been residents of Chapel Hill for several years with Joy teaching preschool and Paul completing work for his doctorate in psychology at the University of North Carolina. When Fassetts' first grandson, Jeffrey Mermin, was born in May 1978, Betty was in Chapel Hill to assist Joy.

Jack and Mimi moved to Maryland after Jack received his doctorate in chemistry from Cornell to accept a position as a member of the chemistry research division of the National Institute of Standards and Technology, which was headquartered in Gaithersburg, just a score of miles north of the nation's capital. Within a few years, they had acquired a home on a large plot of land in Washington Grove, the one-time location of a summer religious camp for Washingtonians. In January 1981, Mimi and Jack presented Betty and Jack with their second grandson, Caleb Fassett. When Betty and Jack made their many hasty automobile trips to Isla during these years, Washington Grove and Chapel Hill were regular stops on the route.

When Jack accepted the position of CEO in 1974, he advised the board of his belief that top executives in electric companies should be relieved at intervals similar to the two-term limit for American presidents. In keeping with a program that would accomplish that goal, in 1980 the board promoted the Yale engineering and Harvard business school's graduate whom Jack had hired early in his tenure as financial vice president to the title of president while Jack remained CEO and became chairman of the board. A year later, also anticipating an early retirement, the Fassetts decided to allow their Old Orchard Road home to be listed by a real estate agent. In short order, a couple who had been admiring the property for some years made an offer that included not only the house, but the large living room rug, the porch furniture, the Franklin stove, and the pool table and accessories Jack had added to the game room. Having other living arrangements available, Betty and Jack accepted the offer.

As part of their move, the Fassetts had a large driveway sale at the Skiff Street entry to their home. Years of accumulated excess furniture and other items were displayed, and most of them sold quickly. Mary Jane Zimmermann assisted Betty in conducting the sale, and that evening Keith and Mary Jane joined Betty and Jack for a lobster dinner at their favorite not-very-fancy restaurant on New Haven harbor to celebrate the event.

*At Electric
Utility
executives'
meeting*

*Surviving a
crash landing
on return
flight home*

NEW YORK POST, THURSDAY, APRIL 9, 1981

72 SAFE IN JFK CRASH-LANDING

Despite its awkward belly-whop landing, Eastern jet winds up with hardly a scratch on it or on any of those aboard at JFK last ni—

By CY EGAN
and DAVID SEIFMAN

Belly-flop pilot is hailed as hero by passengers

A GUTSY Eastern Airlines pilot was hailed as a hero today for dramatically belly-landing his crippled 727 jet at Kennedy Airport without a single injury to the 72 people aboard.

"I've had a lot worse landings with the gear down," Jack Fassett, a passenger, of North Haven, Conn., said of the ordeal last night.

The emergency began when veteran pilot Arthur Glowka discovered the plane's left landing gear would not lower.

Passengers said calm prevailed aboard the plane

— Flight 60 from New Orleans — even when Glowka, after reassuring the passengers over the intercom, said:

"I've been flying 21 years and I've never done this either."

The pilot then set the jet down. It skidded 3000 feet along the runway at 125 miles an hour, trailing a huge spray of sparks. But

there was no fire.

When the jet halted, the passengers and crew quickly walked onto the wings and slid down inflatable chutes to the ground. The evacuation took four minutes.

"He landed so beautifully I want to write him and thank him," said Joseph Boudreau, an oil company executive from New Or-

leans.

While one passengers admitted being "really scared," another said, "The crew was really wonderful. It was a great experience. I have a new appreciation for life."

Glowka decided to make the "hard landing" after he saw the left landing gear would not go down as he approached the airport.

He circled four times, talked by radio to Ea— engineers in Miami trying manually to s— the door housing tha— holding the gear back.

An Eastern spoke— said the crippled plane about 1½ hours of fue— but there was some m— derstanding about — long it would take t— the runway with fire— ant foam.

Estimates for the s— ing operation range— tween one and two h— and Glowka chose h— wait. He retracted all landing gear and too— plane in on its belly.

"He did an except— job," said Eastern's Musto.

Tennis buddies: Andy Wong, Mary Jane Zimmerman, Betty, Mary Tag, Irene Wong

Lora goes to Duke

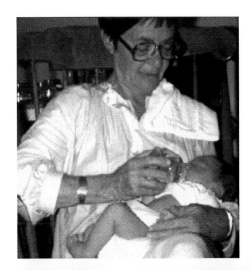

Betty with Grandchildren:
UPPER LEFT: *Jeff, 1978*
UPPER RIGHT: *David, 1981*
MIDDLE LEFT: *Caleb, 1981*
LOWER LEFT: *William, 1983*
LOWER RIGHT: *Grandchildren and Betty reading*

ISLA·DEL·SOL–WINTER 1981

Outside views of condo, Isla del Sol

Living room – dining room view

Betty headed toward the pool

⹀14⹀

MADISON TOWERS AND ISLA DEL SOL, 1982–1985

As part of the much-publicized downtown redevelopment of New Haven, which included construction of a large, enclosed, retail-shopping mall directly across Temple Street from UI's headquarters, two tall apartment buildings were constructed on land between the Yale campus and the Yale–New Haven Hospital. When a two-bedroom tenth-floor apartment in one of those buildings, Madison Towers, was advertised for leasing in early 1982, Jack and Betty decided to abandon the suburbs and experience city living. The apartment was only three blocks from Jack's office where his car could be kept in UI's parking garage, and there was an assigned space for Betty's car in front of the apartment building. Except for driving to the Lawn Club, which was about a mile away, there was little necessity for using a vehicle in the city. Jack could stroll the three blocks back and forth to work and, when in town, he could also enjoy lunch at home. A large new supermarket had been opened between Madison Towers and the hospital. By walking a short distance, Betty could also shop at the mall, visit the shops along Main Street, or even visit Yale's Mellon Art Gallery, which was also on Main Street.

The apartment had a den in addition to its large living room and two bedrooms, but its kitchen was small and its closet space was very limited. Accordingly, instead of moving a lot of furniture from Old Orchard Road, only the basic needs were moved to the apartment in Madison Towers. Most of the Old Orchard Road living room furniture, including the piano, on which Betty had overseen practicing of lessons by all three of the children, and the cherry-wood table that Betty had lovingly refinished, were sent to North Carolina to help to furnish Joy and Paul's house. Betty and Jack toted most of the Old Orchard Road yard equipment, including a rotary mower, a leaf mulcher, and a chain saw, to Washington Grove for Jack to use on his large, wooded lot. Jack's collection of Supreme Court books were moved to Madison Towers, but they were never unpacked there. After reposing in many boxes in the apartment for over a year, Jack donated the collection to the University of Bridgeport Law School, since he had been a trustee of that university for some years and its president was a member of UI's Board of Directors.

Unfortunately, a new series of major crises for UI began developing in early 1983. Oil prices again began skyrocketing, financial markets were in a turmoil over financing of nuclear plants, and a lot of politicians were either paralyzed by developments or again began attacking the regulators and the electric companies. Adding to the problems at UI, the person recently elected president had a severe heart attack, thereby necessitating a revision of Jack's and the board's succession plans. Jack had been elected chairman of NEPOOL in late 1981 and thus was serving in that position as the major crises developed. As recounted in his history of UI, most of his time for the balance of his career as UI CEO was spent overseeing a revival of the Seabrook project after co–lead owner and project manager PSNH had severe financial problems and defaulted on its role on the project. Jack also was supervising teams of engineers and lawyers from NEPOOL, who were negotiating with personnel from Canada's Hydro-Quebec Electric Company regarding purchase by New England of a share of the power to be produced by that company's huge hydroelectric project being constructed near James Bay in northern Quebec. Equally importantly, he was dealing with New England's governors and the regulators in several of the states with respect to utility matters. By strongly supporting the James Bay project, NEPOOL held the support of most of New England's governors (Governor Dukakis of Massachusetts excepted) for its nuclear expansion program and Betty became accustomed to Jack receiving telephone calls during evenings from the Governors of New Hampshire and Vermont, both of whom were closely following developments.

For a period in 1983 and 1984, Jack actually maintained an office in Boston at the headquarters of one of that state's electric companies to facilitate his weekly reviews of construction budgets for the Seabrook project and supervision of other NEPOOL activities. Betty accompanied Jack in two successive years to annual meetings of the New England Conference of Public Utilities Commissioners, which were also attended by regulators from the adjoining Canadian provinces, when Jack was "requested" to make presentations. The first year, at a handy location in suburban Hartford, Jack spoke of power problems and the grave need for completion of the nuclear plant program. The second year, at a resort in Rockport, Maine, Jack reported on the status of the NEPOOL/Hydro-Quebec interconnection project. On that occasion, Betty's mother, who was visiting, accompanied Betty and Jack, first to Burlington, Vermont, where Jack testified before one of that State's regulatory bodies about the proposed heavy transmission line through Vermont that was required to bring anticipated James Bay power to a connection with the NEPOOL power grid. Thereafter, the threesome had a scenic ride to two days of meetings in Maine.

In 1983, Lora opted to spend a college year as a Duke exchange student at McGill University in Montreal, Canada. Her choice involved her parents in making two trips to the city where they had spent their brief honeymoon thirty-six years earlier. During a stay of several days on one visit, Betty and Jack toured many of the sights of the city that they had made no effort to see in 1947. They once again enjoyed some fine French cooking and they revisited the site of the Montreal World's Fair, to which they had taken Jack's parents over a long summer weekend years before. After Jack's father had died, Jack's mother had moved from Stamford to live with Jack's sister and her husband in New City, New York, and she died there in 1981.

The Fassetts' plan upon leaving Old Orchard Road was to retain the Madison Towers apartment for the year or two remaining until Jack could retire from full-time employment at UI. Their plan was to then make Florida their primary residence. Since the Isla condo was not adequate for their retirement desires, on one visit to the condo in 1983, Betty and Jack made a survey of the real estate market in the St. Petersburg area and, after consulting with a builder, concluded that they could build a new home to their own specifications for no more than it would cost for an acceptable established property. As a result, through the builder, they bought a small plot of land on an island one bridge south of Isla and retained the builder to construct their planned retirement home. Starting in late 1983 and continuing well into 1984, Betty spent considerable time at the Isla condo observing and overseeing the construction of their Tierra Verde home.

Isla had a tennis club with six clay courts where Betty soon became involved with a group of women players and Jack never had any trouble finding eager male opponents when he was able to visit the condo. Both Betty and Jack were able to be in residence during the week in October 1983 when the club championships were being held, so Jack entered the men's singles and together they entered the mixed doubles. As a result, they added two plaques to their collection by winning both titles. Most of the residents of Isla were "snowbirds," which meant there was a lot going on during the winter months. However, things grew more quiet during the off-season, and Betty and Jack found that they particularly enjoyed the area during those quieter months since there were no lines to enter restaurants, there were a lot of early-bird specials, and the traffic was much less of a problem.

While Betty was "supervising" construction in Florida, Jack continued to be extremely busy in New Haven, Hartford (Connecticut regulatory agencies), Westboro (NEPOOL matters), New York City (financing matters), Boston (Seabrook construction meetings), and in Seabrook (on-site inspections). With considerable support from both Governor John Sununu of New Hampshire, who even met with Jack on a couple of Sundays, and federal energy officials, the Seabrook project was reactivated and moving forward by mid-1984. Accordingly, it was possible for Jack to revive his retirement agreement with UI's board, although two years later than originally planned.

While Jack formally retired on January 1, 1985, he agreed to work full-time until his successor as CEO, chosen by the board (actually, by a committee of the board headed by Jack), had begun work and had been given a period of orientation by Jack. That successor, initially interviewed by Jack at the condo on Isla, was a young, former executive vice president of Georgia Power Company. He assumed the office of president and CEO of UI on April 1, 1985, and Jack accompanied him to all meetings of NEPOOL and the Seabrook owners for several months.

During that transition period, all of the top executives of the New England utilities, together with all of New England's Governors and many of the region's regulators, assembled in the famed Faneuil Hall in Boston, joined by Canada's Energy Minister, the Premier of Quebec, and a number of federal representatives, for the formal signing of the NEPOOL/Hydro-Quebec James Bay Agreement. All of the governors, the energy minister, and Jack made speeches and, in the glare of television, Jack and Hydro-Quebec's president ceremoniously signed an impressive document. In fact, the actual agreement had been executed in the presence of the lawyers for both parties earlier. Being busy in Florida, Betty missed the big occasion and the reception given at Hotel Meridien thereafter, but videos were made so she and the rest of the family got to hear all of the congratulatory speeches.

When Jack's successor at UI and his family got settled in Connecticut and he had become acclimated to his role at the company, Jack terminated the lease for the Madison Towers apartment and became a formal domiciliary of Florida. During his last few months using the apartment, while commuting regularly between Tampa and Hartford, Jack slept on the Hideabed, which he and Betty had transported since their original residence on Seneca Parkway in Rochester. He often ate takeout dinners while riding an exercise bicycle and watching programs on TV. Upon termination of the lease, Jack drove to Florida and carried the exercise bike and the TV set there, but the heavy Hideabed and the few other items in the apartment were donated to the building's superintendent. Much to Jack's surprise, just prior to his departure, he was visited by the New Haven Alderrman from the downtown district who presented a copy of a resolution, passed by the Board of Aldermen, thanking Jack for his efforts on behalf of the city and wishing him good health in his retirement.

Guy Coulombe, Hydro-Quebec president, seated left, and John Fassett, chairman of the New England Power Pool executive committee, shake hands after signing agreements for New England states to acquire electric hydropower from Quebec. Participating, from left, are: Rhode Island Gov. Joseph Garrahy; Yves Duhaime, Quebec minister of energy and resources; Vermont Gov. Richard Snelling; Rene Levesque, prime minister of Quebec; Connecticut Gov. William O'Neill, and Maine Gov. Joseph Brennan.

CANADA WILL SUPPLY POWER
Electric pool to aid region

BOSTON (AP) — A $324 million network linking New England and Quebec will begin supplying the six states with cheap Canadian electricity in the fall of 1986, officials say.

An 11-year contract between Hydro-Quebec of Canada and the 64 electric companies that comprise the New England Power Pool was signed Monday in bilingual ceremonies at Faneuil Hall.

The plan is expected to save New Englanders more than $100 million a year, and is expected to bring in more than $5 billion in revenues to Quebec.

ty, and two-thirds of it will be priced at 80 percent of NEPOOL's average fossil fuel cost.

"It's just the beginning," Levesque said. "We all know there's a promise of substantial further development in this agreement."

Yves Duhaime, Quebec's energy minister, said the agreement, which a Hydro-Quebec official called "a real good neighbor understanding," provides "a permanent link between Quebec and New England — a link which as you know could be increased from 690 megawatts to 2,000 megawatts."

He predicted, "I am confident if

The power partnership is expected to save New Englanders more than 5 million barrels of oil a year, and Vermont Gov. Richard A. Snelling said it represents a plan to free New England from its substantial dependence on foreign oil.

Rhode Island Gov. J. Joseph Garrahy added, "It's an historic day that provides the foundation of energy security and economic vitality for our region."

Maine Gov. Joseph E. Brennan noted the contract means $8 to $9 million in annual savings initially for his state, and he said, "Where I come from that's still serious money."

*Madison Towers, 111 Park Street
New Haven*

Jack works to secure power-sharing agreement with president of Hydro-Quebec, 1985

*Supervising
construction of
new house on
Tierra Verde*

*Construction site
of pool and Jacuzzi,
Tierra Verde*

Visit to Brentwood, 1984 (left to right) Mug, Mary, Blanche, Betty, Lo

⁓15⁓

TIERRA VERDE, 1984–1989

Tierra Verde actually consisted of three sand keys which were opened to development when the state constructed a toll bridge and highway, with several additional shorter bridges, to permit automobile access to Fort Desoto State Park. The park was a fine, large facility containing several sandy beaches, a large picnic grove, and a camping area with access to the water for campers' boats. It also contained Old Fort Desoto, a historic site, which had been constructed at the outset of the Spanish-American War to guard the entry to Tampa Bay. The Fassetts' home was located on Entrada, the first of the Tierra Keys. It consisted of a living/dining room with a raised brick fireplace, a kitchen, two bedrooms, two bathrooms, a den, a large sun room with sliding glass doors to the screen-enclosed swimming pool and spa, and a large garage. The cement-block house was finished with tan stucco, and the roof was red tiles upon the rear of which resided several large solar-heating panels and a tank that provided hot water for the residence. For privacy, Betty had a solid, also tan-stuccoed. five-foot wall constructed to enclose the backyard, including the pool facilities.

The key upon which the house was constructed once was home to a variety of wildlife, and one part had been a nesting area for exotic birds. However, most of the animals and birds had evacuated when the key was bulkheaded and filled with sand dredged from adjacent waters. Since the Fassett home was one of the first on the southern end of Entrada, for a couple of years their yard was periodically visited by raccoons, large turtles, and, on one occasion, by a six-foot-long black snake. For several years, some birds still attempted to nest in their old habitat and, when Betty and Jack would ride their bicycles to the end of the key, vigilant birds guarding the nests would seek to drive the intruders away. During their first few years on Entrada, Betty and Jack made frequent use of the three-speed bicycles that had been purchased to ride into town from Smith Point while on Nantucket. They even, on several occasions, took the several-mile ride to Fort Desoto.

Betty and Jack became members of Lakewood Country Club on the mainland in order to use its excellent tennis facilities (although it was primarily a golfer's club) and dining room. However, they also continued to play on the courts at Isla, and Jack successfully defended his men's singles title in 1984, 1985, and 1986. A year after the Fassetts became settled on Tierra, Jack's sister, Connie, and her husband, Gunnar, after several visits, decided to have a similar abode built on a lot a short block away from the Fassetts. Upon Gunnar's retirement from his position as a research biologist at Lederle Labs of American Cyanamid Company and Connie's from her New York City job doing artwork for Simplicity Patterns, the Redins also retired to Tierra. The Redins hired the builder who had constructed the Fassett home and Betty again served as "superintendent" of the construction project. Betty, Connie, Gunnar, and Jack were the closest of friends, eating and socializing together regularly while the Fassetts lived in Florida.

With Jack commuting to New Haven for two days each month attending board meetings (since Jack was senior director, the bank accommodated his schedule by setting its board meetings for the day following UI's; Jack retired from all other boards), Betty was fully occupied tending to her new home, playing tennis, enjoying bridge games, and occasionally joining Jack fishing in the channel across the street from their home. For his first few years on Tierra, Jack's routine while in Florida was to play tennis in the morning, go fishing in the afternoon, and spend most evenings in his den writing the history of UI that his fellow directors had importuned him to produce. A great variety of fish, and even a few manatee, occasionally traversed Entrada's channel with the changing tides and Jack caught lots of whiting, some flounder, a few redfish, drum and grouper, many inedible catfish, and, on one occasion, a four-foot hammerhead shark, which he immediately brought to the sundeck doors so Betty's bridge companions could be startled by it. Jack fed some of his catch to the prolific herons and ducks who watched him fish, and one large blue heron regularly awaited his arrival with his fishing gear and stood nearby awaiting a feeding. Betty accused Jack of having conversations with the friendly bird.

Betty's primary interest with respect to the yard was grapefruit trees. While the house was under construction, Betty told the builder she desired a grapefruit tree in the front yard to accompany the live oak and several large palms that had survived the filling of the key. When she later first inspected the landscaping, there was a feeble tree in the center of the front yard containing a single grapefruit that she initially thought was plastic. In short order, that tree was moved to the side yard where it grew to be large, but produced only sour, lemonlike fruit (good only for sour drinks). However, over the first few years, three larger grapefruit trees of different varieties and a key-lime tree were planted in the rear yard, and all prospered with fertilization despite the sandy soil.

Betty generally eschewed singles tennis games, but she had an abundance of doubles matches at Lakewood. Within a short time, despite being somewhat older than most members, she was asked to join the club's women's team that played matches against other clubs in a wide area. As a result of her reputation as a tough net player, her teammates presented her with a shirt inscribed "Mean Betty Jean," which she still prizes. She had only one gap in playing which occurred when she broke a bone in her foot in the course of a game. Fortuitously, an orthopedist was playing nearby and rushed her to his office for an X-ray and to apply a cast. Jack played a lot of tennis at both Isla and Lakewood, but also traveled to numerous seniors' tournaments, mostly on Florida's west coast. In 1988, he played in the men's singles tournament at Lakewood and reached the finals where he was beaten by a courteous twenty-five-year-old who congratulated each of Jack's good shots with "Nice shot, sir." A large contingent of female and male senior members of the club turned out to view that unusual event.

Betty's regular bridge groups comprised a mixture of old friends from Isla, new friends from Lakewood, and a few other new residents on Tierra. The number of Tierra neighbors increased rapidly as virtually all of the available lots on the key were filled with new homes, some of them very large, within a few years.

With its great weather, Florida attracted lots of visitors, and the Fassetts enjoyed their share during their days on Tierra. For the first couple of years after moving to the key, the Fassetts retained their Isla condo and rented it on a seasonal basis. However, after experiencing destructive tenants and rent-collection problems, Betty decided she did not like being a landlady and the condo was sold. In the interim, however, it did serve as an extended honeymoon site for Lora and her husband after their marriage in the Duke Chapel in Durham, North Carolina, in May 1986. Lora and Parker chose to be married at Duke since all of their friends, sorority sisters, and fraternity brothers were there, and they were strangers in the Fassetts' new area. They were wed as Lora was completing work for an MBA degree with concentration in hospital management and Parker was finishing at Duke Law School. Lora selected the spacious clubhouse of a suburban Durham club, Croasdaile Country Club, for the reception. The event attracted many branches of the Fassett and Mason clans, as well as many Duke students, and was a roaring success. Betty and Jack returned to Durham in May 1987, to attend the graduations of both of the newlyweds.

Among the visitors Betty and Jack enjoyed seeing occasionally on Tierra were Rusty and Bob Hart, who had retired to a small community, Floral City, in central Florida. Ray and Chick Rapp also visited from California and, shortly after settling in Florida, Betty discovered that her other close army pal, Peg Lindo, was residing in St. Petersburg with her retired-general husband, Bill Yamber. The Yambers also had an abode (a large, permanently-sited trailer) in Cherokee, North Carolina, and when the Fassetts traveled to Asheville and Highland Falls (where Isla's tennis pro worked during summers; he and his wife hosted the Fassetts there) for Jack to compete in tournaments a couple of summers, they also visited with Peg and Bill. Betty often accompanied Jack to United States Tennis Association–sanctioned tennis tournaments in which he competed in Florida and elsewhere, thus getting to know the other regular participants' wives. She enjoyed cheering for Jack during matches and the usual nice welcoming dinners for the contenders, but she did not enjoy the delays between matches nor missing her own games.

With Florida's sunshine and seashore and their grandparent's swimming pool and nearby tennis courts as lures, Joy and Paul and their two sons, Jeffrey and David, and Jack and Mimi and their two sons, Caleb and William, all managed to visit Tierra on numerous occasions during the old folks' Tierra years. (Betty had been in Chapel Hill to assist Joy at the times of birth of Jeffrey in 1978 and David in 1981, and she and Jack had also visited Washington Grove following the arrivals of those grandsons in 1980 and 1983). During the summer, tennis camps were run at the Lakewood Club, and during several summer visits, Betty enrolled the young visitors for a week of camp. She also would hit balls back and forth across the net with any willing grandson and all of them were willing to a degree, but William was eager to hit as long as his grandmother was willing to do so.

During his years as a director of EEI, which sponsored an exhibit about the electric industry at Epcot in Orlando, Jack had a VIP pass good to admit him and several guests to the attraction. The pass was well used during visits by the grandchildren, and they also liked to travel with their grandparents to the closer Busch Gardens in Tampa, which featured an impressive wild-animal range, a rafting ride on a man-made turbulent stream, a simulated trip into outer space, and many other attractions.

Not having had an extended vacation since Jack joined UI, Betty and Jack decided upon his retirement to catch up by taking, on an every-other-year schedule, some of the foreign trips to which they had aspired. Both agreed on England and Scotland for their first destination, and in 1985, they booked a three-week tour for late June and early July with a tour guide recommended by their travel agency. It was a great adventure. The small group had multiday stays in London on both ends (Westminster Cathedral, London Bridge and Tower, Downing Street, and Buckingham Palace at the changing of the guard were prime attractions), and stays in Chester (where they walked the old Roman wall), Lake Windemere (where they took a ride on the lake), Glasgow, Edinburgh (where another changing of the guard was viewed at the castle), and Gleneagles (a plush golf resort in Scotland where a celebration was in progress with all of the attending men in traditional kilt attire). En route visits were made to Hampton Court, Windsor Castle, Shakespeare's cottage in Stratford, Loch Lomond, Durham Cathedral, York Minster, and King's College in Cambridge. With a knowledgeable tour guide and a small group, it was a most enjoyable venture into European travel with two also memorable sidelights. Just after arriving in Chester, a telephone call was received from Tierra Verde advising that a hurricane had struck Florida and had taken down the recently installed pool enclosure, blown many tiles off the roof, and somehow ruptured a water line. A kindly neighbor had managed to shut off the water at the street, and the caller sought instructions for further action. Jack demurred that there was nothing he could do from England and directed that his builder be contacted to restore the damage. When the group reached Gleneagles, three other couples in the group, all golfers, importuned the guide to arrange a side trip to St. Andrews, a few hours away on the coast. Since the guide advised that it would take at least eight to justify such a jaunt, Betty and Jack volunteered to go along. It was a scenic ride along the rocky coast and, while the others played some golf, the Fassetts walked a couple of the holes on the rugged course and then retreated to the town to visit some shops and a typical Scottish pub.

Departing in late August 1987, Betty and Jack left for their second and longest European tour, this time to France. After a couple of days visiting Parisian sights, the coach-load of American tourists proceeded to see Reims Cathedral (close to the site of the first location of the 134th Hospital in 1944), and then to Troyes and Dijon for sightseeing before stopping in Geneva, Switzerland, on Lake Geneva, for a stay. There they visited the international headquarters of both the Red Cross and the United Nations and took a ride on the lake. Following that brief detour from France, the coach proceeded to Grenoble (scene of the 1968 Winter Olympics) for a night before crossing the French Alps to the Mediterranean coast. There the group spent several days in Cannes (scene of Betty's R & R in 1945 at the end of the war) with side trips to Nice and an evening at the Casino in Monte Carlo. While the Fassetts did not attempt to be cleared (a credit check was required) to enter the main gambling room, Betty enjoyed herself immensely in the adjacent room containing hundreds of one-arm bandits. In the course of the evening, she won enough francs to treat the entire group to a round of drinks in a bar adjoining the casino before they returned to Cannes. While proceeding to overnight stops in Nimes and Toulouse, the group visited many intriguing sights, including the ancient Papal Palace in Avignon and the walled city of Carcassonne. During a two-day stay in Lourdes, Betty saw the location of the claimed healing waters, and she and Jack watched the depressing sight one evening of a long parade of sick and disabled people heading to the cathedral seeking miracles. Reaching the Atlantic coast, during a day in Biarritz, surfers were viewed riding the waves at the shore of the city that once was the favorite resort of wealthy Britishers. After visiting Bordeaux, the coach took a side-trip to Cognac to tour that area's famous liquor facilities. Another stop was made at the historic battle location in Poitiers before reaching Tours. Tours was the group's sleeping location as additional side-trips were made to visit the famed Loire castles: Chambord, Cheverney, Amboise, and Chenonceau. Another Loire castle also was visited in Angiers before again reaching the coast for a hike out to Mont St. Michel and a day of wandering around that ancient marvel of a castle on an island in the tidal bay. Before returning to Paris for visits to Chartres and Versailles and an evening visiting nightspots in Montmartre, the group visited all of the D-day landing sites in Normandy, the town of St. Lo, and the massive, and, especially for WWII veterans, breathtaking Normandy American Cemetery and Memorial which covers over two hundred acres and is the final resting place for over ten thousand American casualties of the invasion.

Betty returned to Tierra drained by the long journey of over twenty-five hundred miles in France and the plane flights, but inspired by the slices of history and geography she had viewed. The Fassetts' journey to Germany in late May and early June 1989 involved somewhat less time and mileage, but it encompassed more of the areas Betty had seen, mostly from the back of an army truck, during the final American drive to victory in 1945. Flying into Frankfurt, the modest-sized Brendan Tours group was bused to Rudesheim where they boarded a Rhine River cruise ship. They passed the Lorelei Rock and the remains of the bridge at Remagen before debarking in the cathedral city of Cologne. After a day wandering that city and its cathedral, the tour's coach arrived to proceed to Hamburg with a midday stop in Hamelin, famous for its pied piper and its beautiful gardens. From Hamburg, the coach, with a very skittish driver traveling at a very modest speed and always watching his rearview mirror due to severe restrictions imposed by the Russians on traversing the Autobahn, proceeded to isolated Berlin. Arriving in West Berlin, the group settled in Hotel Hamburg and visited the West German city's many sights, including the Reichstag, Charlottenburg Castle, and the 1936 Olympics Stadium. The main event of this visit was a crossing of the still-intact Berlin Wall at Checkpoint Charlie (where everyone was carefully screened, the coach was thoroughly searched both underneath and inside, and a special East German guide came aboard to provide a Communist interpretation of the sights) and a tour of East Berlin's many sights. Particular emphasis by the guide was placed on the impressive Russian War Memorial where Russia's costly war effort against Nazi Germany was extolled.

Leaving West Berlin, the Russian-controlled Autobahn passed near both Halle (where Betty's 134th had been located as WWII ended) and Leipzig (from which Jack's maternal grandmother had emigrated as a young girl), but, again, no diversion from the highway was permitted. After Berlin, overnight visits were made to Nuremberg (visiting both the old city and Hitler's stadium) and Rothenburg before spending several days in Munich. A joyous evening at the Hofbau Haus and a day viewing the city's sights were offset by a trip to Dachau to view the grim remains of that deadly concentration camp. The latter part of the tour encompassed the German Alps, Freiberg, Oberamagau, and Lake Constance, with visits to the dramatic Lindenhof and Neuschwanstein Castles. Final visits were to Heidelberg, the Black Forest, and the once-famous resort at Baden Baden before arrival in Frankfurt for the return trip to Tierra Verde to relax following the arduous journey.

House at Tierra Verde

Growing grapefruit

Hydroponic tomatoes

*Betty and Jack
with bicycles*

*David, Joy and Jeff
in the pool with Betty
watching while tennis
clothes dry on the line*

*Betty and Connie
enjoying the Jacuzzi*

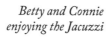

*Betty fishing in the channel across
from house; the catch is good*

*Betty's Lakewood foursome
playing at Lakewood, Blanche watching*

Christmas on Tierra Verde
UPPER LEFT: *Betty with grandsons*
ABOVE: *Jack, William, Mimi, Caleb*
MIDDLE LEFT: *Betty gives tennis lessons to Caleb and William*

Betty at Epcot

Jack and Betty at Busch Gardens, Tampa, with Jeff, David and Joy

Trip to England and Scotland
ABOVE: *Betty viewing London Bridge*
LEFT: *Betty with the guard at Edinburgh Castle*

Trips to France and Germany
TOP: *Cemetery at Normandy*
MID LEFT: *Lourdes*
MID RIGHT: *Cannes*
LOWER LEFT: *Munich*
LOWER RIGHT: *Baden-Baden*

Lora and Parker marry at Duke Chapel

TOP: *After the wedding, on the steps of Duke Chapel*
ABOVE LEFT: *Parker and Betty dance at the wedding*
RIGHT: *Betty with Lora and Parker at their graduations,*
May 1986

~16~

TIERRA VERDE, 1990–1993

By the time of UI's annual meeting in 1990, Jack had completed researching (done in company archives during visits and his own records) and writing (all of the word processing was done by his successor's able secretary, who volunteered to decipher the handwritten chapters delivered each month) his history of UI. (It was published in 1991 and widely distributed in the industry by UI.) Before embarking on his second writing venture (a biography of Supreme Court Justice Stanley Reed), which he had been contemplating since encouraged to do so by the editor of the *Journal of Supreme Court History* (shortly after his retirement Jack had written an article about Justice Reed and the school segregation cases that had been published in the *Journal*), Betty chose Ireland for their next tour, and they decided not to wait two years for the trip.

Departing from Tampa on their forty-third anniversary (August 4, 1990), the Fassetts arrived in Limerick where they joined their Brendan Tours group the following day. Heading toward Oughterard, stops were made at Bunratty Castle and Folk Park, the Cliffs of Moher, and Galway Cathedral before arriving at an inn on Galway Bay. During the following day, a boat trip was taken to the largest of the Aran Islands, Innismore, which was like visiting a culture of a former century. Next were stops at the marble factory in Connemara and at the Irish counterpart to Lourdes as the group proceeded to the Irish resort town of Ballyshannon on Donegal Bay. During the stay at the resort, the guide, a vivacious middle-aged schoolteacher on summer vacation, inquired whether anyone would be interested in accompanying him on an evening visit to a local pub. Betty and Jack accepted and had a great experience. It was a Friday night and the pub was busy with many families, including young children. The proprietor was emceeing what amounted to a local talent contest with many people singing, playing instruments, or telling jokes. After some time, she importuned the guide (who obviously was a close friend) to sing and he proved to be a fine Irish tenor. With that knowledge, the group had the pleasure of hearing him perform several times while traveling during the balance of the tour. After exploring the rugged wilds of Donegal, the coach backtracked and took the cross-island trip to Dublin on the Irish Sea. During several days in the capital, a play was attended, St. Patrick's Cathedral was visited, hours were spent in the Trinity College Library where the Book of Kells is displayed, and a day was allowed for just wandering around the interesting city. A side-trip north from Dublin to the Boyne Valley permitted exploration of many intriguing pre-Christian archaeological sites. From Dublin, the coach proceeded along the coast to Waterford, where the group stayed and took a tour of the cut-glass factory. Then it was again across the island and County Cork, with a visit to the old stone castle where both Betty and Jack lay on their backs and kissed the blarney stone (the stupidest thing she ever did, according to Betty), to a couple of days of circling the Ring of Kerry and the Dingle Peninsula from quarters in Killarney and Tralee before returning to Shannon Airport for the trip home.

Despite covering so much of the island, and doing some hasty research at Trinity's library, the Fassetts never did find the location of Castle Fassett (they did find that every old stone structure on the island was sometimes called a castle), the place where Jack's Scottish ancestor was imprisoned by the victorious British when he supported Charles II in 1651. He took the name of the castle when an act of Parliament later allowed the prisoners to emigrate to Massachusetts. While a student at Brown University, son Jack became an ardent collector of ancient gravestone rubbings. He found the weathered stone of the original American Fassett (on the stone, Patrick Fasset was spelled with one t; he died November 7, 1713) in an old cemetery in Billerica, Massachusetts, and made a rubbing which has since occupied a spot on one of the walls of Fassetts' residences.

In 1991, his first year in the sixty-five and over seniors' category, Jack was qualified to play in the United States Tennis Association Senior National Tournament which was held in Little Rock, Arkansas. Betty chose not to take that long ride, but she joined Jack in participating in the Florida tryouts for the Senior Olympics and, that summer, accompanied him to those championships which were held on the campus of Syracuse University in New York state. That trip was expanded to include stays in Hamden, Connecticut, with Andy and Irene Wong (where they visited the collection of books Jack had donated at Quinnipiack Law School, which had acquired Bridgeport Law School) and in Ridgefield, Connecticut, with Jack's younger sister and her family. After the Olympics, where Jack and Andy Chau were beaten in the semifinals, the Fassetts also visited friends in Rochester and rode around the expanded University of Rochester campus before returning to Tierra Verde.

During her last years on Tierra, while Betty enjoyed her impressive grove of citrus trees, her regular tennis games at the Lakewood Club, many bridge games, and, most of all, visits to or from the children and their growing families, Jack concentrated on producing the 771-page tome titled *New Deal Justice: The Life of Stanley Reed of Kentucky*. A considerable amount of Jack's research was done at the main Yale Library (it had tapes of old newspapers and many other pertinent records) during the monthly New Haven trips and a lot at the law library of Stetson Law School, which was located only a few miles from Tierra in St. Petersburg. Jack was fortunate that the very competent secretary to the *Stetson Law Review* agreed to undertake the chore of converting the yellow pages of handwritten drafts of chapters that Jack was producing, first into clean drafts and then into an edited manuscript. At the outset, Jack assumed it would be a modest-length book because Justice Reed had told him that he proposed to destroy most of his records when he retired.

However, in the course of research, Jack found that the justice, in fact, had destroyed only the records pertinent to his proposed dissent in the school segregation cases and that, upon the justice's death, his sons had donated all of his papers to the University of Kentucky. Chasing down the lead, in the fall of 1991, after Betty and Jack visited her mother—who had lived with Betty's sister, Mildred, and her husband since Dutch's death—and her other sisters, living in the Pittsburgh suburbs, the Fassetts proceeded to Lexington, Kentucky, home of that state's university. Heartily welcomed by librarians at the archives of the university library, Jack spent several days perusing the Reed papers. He selected a couple or thousand pages to be Xeroxed for use in Tierra. Betty became an expert at copying all varieties of documents on a Xerox machine that the librarians designated for her private use during the stay. A year later, Betty and Jack returned by air (Tampa to Cincinnati; small plane to Lexington) to repeat the process on the more than 378 boxes of materials in the archive collection.

Also in September 1992, Jack drove Betty to Pittsburgh so that she could attend the fiftieth reunion of her nursing school class. The reunion featured a tour of Allegheny General Hospital and a cruise by the group on the Ohio River. While seven of her classmates were deceased, about two dozen returned for the nostalgic get-together. The final manuscript of Jack's book went to the publisher in early 1994 and the book was released later that year, much to Betty's relief that Jack would not be spending almost every afternoon and many evenings busy writing in his den.

With the demands of Jack's writing and other commitments, Betty opted that they not undertake a summer European vacation in 1991. Instead, the Fassetts stayed on the North American continent by scheduling a visit to Seattle followed by an early August tour of Alaska. By then, Lora and Parker had moved from their original post-Duke home and jobs in Charlotte, North Carolina, to Seattle, Washington, where Parker was associated with a large law firm and Lora was employed as an aide to an executive at one of the nation's largest HMOs, Puget Sound HMO. The land tour conducted by Westours was preceded by a cruise on Holland-America's M.S. *Westerdam* from Vancouver, through the inside passage, to Skagway with stops in Ketchikan and Juneau. The enjoyable, smooth cruise largely cured Betty of her deep-seated fear of the seas which she had developed during her two crossings of the Atlantic in the army during the war. It thus permitted the Fassetts to consider future cruises as alternatives to land tours. In Ketchikan, the group visited Totem Bight Park with its artifacts of early-day Alaska, and in Juneau they viewed the imposing Mendenhall Glacier. The intimate size of the group (nine tourists with one guide and, eventually, one driver) made both the traveling and sightseeing exceedingly comfortable. Leaving the Westerdam in Skagway, the group visited the National Historical Park devoted to the events of the gold-rush days and then made the steep, rickety ascent to the summit of White Pass in a car of the ancient White Horse and Yukon Railroad. During several days in White Horse and Dawson City, the group panned for gold at an abandoned mine, visited the cabin of poet Robert Service and heard a recitation of his poems, visited a wildlife preserve, and enjoyed Alaskan-style food and entertainment. From Dawson City, the group embarked on the vessel Yukon Queen for a daylong cruise north on the Yukon River through rugged country where elk were seen bathing in the river and eagles flew overhead. Debarking in Eagle (population 180), established as a northern outpost for the air corps during WWII and thus having a good landing strip, the small group boarded a chartered plane for the short flight over the mountains to Fairbanks. During a stay in that interesting northern city, the group went on a stern-wheeler steamboat to an Athabascan village where all aspects of native culture (including salmon-drying and sled-dog training) were observed.

Fairbanks to Denali (Mount McKinley) was by a much more modern railroad with a dining car. During a couple of days quartered in a comfortable cabin in Denali National Park, a raft trip was experienced in the rapid-flowing stream at the mountain's base, and a bus trip (in a yellow school bus diverted to carry tourists during the summer) was taken up the steep, winding dirt road toward the snow-covered peak. The viewing was fabulous with a great variety of wild animals. The bus driver said the group was lucky because the trip was the first one he had made that summer where the weather permitted clear views of the peak. After Dinali, it was anticlimactic to stay in Anchorage (even the trip on Portage Lake to view another glacier was anticlimactic) prior to flying back to Seattle for a further visit with Lora and Parker and another flight back to Tampa. Betty always said the Alaskan trip was the one she would most like to repeat.

As Betty passed her seventieth birthday, her energy decreased significantly and her ability to play extended tennis matches waned. Except for a hospital stay and a relatively brief recovery period for a hysterectomy performed at Yale–New Haven Hospital in 1970 by Dr. Billings (who previously had delivered Lora), arthroscopic knee surgery performed in an outpatient facility in the same city (which only interrupted her tennis for a month or so), and periods with her wrist in a cast after she stepped on a tennis ball that rolled on to her court from an adjacent court in New Haven and her foot in a cast as a result of her mishap at Lakewood, Betty had been quite healthy since being married. However, she and Jack now decided that it was becoming time to cease facing the problems of maintaining a house, a swimming pool, and a yard with its citrus trees and to seek a quieter lifestyle. A number of Betty and Jack's friends resided in a gated, senior (over fifty-five) community consisting of six high-rise condominium buildings called Point Brittany located on an isle between Isla and the interstate highway approach to the Sunshine Skyway Bridge, a toll bridge spanning the entry to Tampa Bay. Among their friends were Jack's tennis partner and his wife, both retired physicians, who had shared the Senior Olympics' experience in Syracuse and who had traveled with the Fassetts to Fort Lauderdale one year with the team that represented Lakewood Club in the state championships. Having been alerted by Doctor Chau of an anticipated vacancy in their building, Jack made an offer in late 1992. It was accepted, and Betty prepared to have a giant garage sale on Tierra in anticipation of downsizing again as a contract was being negotiated for the sale of that property.

The year before making the significant move to the senior community, Betty and Jack undertook one additional European trip. On June 3, 1992, using some of the many frequent flyer miles he had built up by his monthly commuting from Tampa to New York, Betty and Jack flew first-class from Tampa to New York and from there to Zurich, Switzerland, where they commenced a tour of that Alpine country and a cruise down the Rhine River to Amsterdam in the Netherlands. After a sightseeing tour of Zurich, the tour coach drove along Lake Wales to deliver the tourists to Verduz in the small principality of Liechtenstein, where the ancient castle and relatively modern town were explored. Thence, the coach traversed the rugged Alps of Heidi country through the Julien Pass to St. Moritz, viewing some of the most picturesque scenery the Fassetts had ever seen. From that famous skiing area, the coach crossed into Italy for a short visit on Lake Como and a ferry ride across Lake Maggiore. From Stresa, the group took a small boat for a bumpy ride to Isla Bella (the ride was so bumpy that Jack lost into the lake while trying to get a good photo of the onetime home of the cardinals the Argus camera he had purchased at Fort Monroe). Departing Italy to return to Switzerland by the Simplon Pass, the coach delivered the group to Tasch to take the short mountain-train ride to Zermatt and a stay in one of the rustic chalets beneath the Matterhorn. Among the activities at Zermatt was a ride on the rack-railway to the top of 10,272-foot Gornegut for a breathtaking, panoramic view of the Swiss Alps and the taking of a photo of the tour group.

After the mountains, the coach traversed the vineyards and groves of the Rhone River valley to Lake Geneva, Berne, Lucerne (where Jack was finally able to purchase a replacement camera in a co-op store), and Basle, whence the Fassetts boarded the M.S. *Italia* for the cruise down the Rhine to Holland. It was a relaxing trip through many locks, passing much other river traffic and many picturesque towns and castles (as well as several nuclear generating plants), with sightseeing stops in Strasbourg, Boppard, and Cologne before arrival in Nijimegen, Holland, for transfer to a hotel in a suburb of Amsterdam. From that location, Betty and Jack took the trolley a couple of days to tour the sights of Amsterdam, including one area reeking of the permissive Dutch drug culture, before returning to Tierra and continuing arrangements for the move to Point Brittany.

Despite the turmoil of moving, Betty and Jack were able to schedule one last shorter trip before their 1993 move. Having recently visited Alaska, they decided to complete their record and visit the other noncontiguous state, Hawaii, during the spring. Having received good reports about Tauck Tours, a Connecticut tour company, Jack booked a thirteen-day, four-island tour with that operator, and it certainly lived up to its excellent reputation. Although the tour group (forty plus the guide and driver) was much larger than any previously experienced, no long coach trips were involved, and all of the accommodations and arrangements were first-class. The group assembled and spent their first three days at the Royal Hawaiian Hotel on Waikiki Beach on Oahu. On the first full day of the tour, the group went to Pearl Harbor and visited (by boat) the U.S.S. *Arizona* Memorial and the nearby U.S.S. *Bowfin* Submarine Museum and Park and then the Bishop Museum with its many exhibits of Hawaiian history and culture. Near the entry to the Bishop Museum stood a huge, old tree that was dropping kola nuts. At Betty's suggestion, Jack gathered a few of the hard-shelled nuts and saved them to take back to Tierra where they were put in two pots in the pool enclosure where she nursed hydroponically grown tomato plants. In short order, two sprouts were growing and, when the Fassetts moved to Point Brittany, their doctor neighbor claimed the infant trees for planting in his yard.

While the tour was originally supposed to go next on a visit to Kauai, the itinerary had to be altered because a hurricane had ravaged the planned facility. Instead, the group was treated to a day and night on the less-populated island of Molokai, location of the famous leper colony and of large macadamia nut groves. The former was only viewed from a high cliff overlooking its secluded cove, but the group actually participated in the harvesting of some macadamias at one of the groves.

Having been denied Kauai, the group's initial stay on Maui and the stay on the big island (Hawaii) were extended to three full days each which permitted longer explorations of them. From Lahaina, Maui's historic whaling port, a small boat trip was taken to observe the whales, which congregate offshore, and, while some in the group played golf, Betty and Jack went shopping and purchased matching Hawaiian attire to wear to a scheduled luau. On Hawaii, one day was spent at Volcano National Park viewing exhibits and walking across areas of still-warm lava and steam vents. An exciting helicopter ride, during which Betty rode in the copilot's seat, was taken up a lush valley to near the top of Mauna Kea. Once again boarding one of Hawaiian Airlines island-hopping planes, the group returned to Maui, this time staying at the Four Seasons Resort for a couple of days on the beach, at the pool, relaxing, and playing tennis with loaned equipment.

*Betty at
Bunratty Folk
Park, Ireland*

Jack, Jr. at "Fasset" gravestone

*Visiting an ancient
Irish monastery,
Mellifont Abbey*

Betty and Jack in front of glacier at Portage Lake near Anchorage, Alaska

Betty and Guide at poet Robert Service's cabin

Betty at abandoned gold mine, Dawson City, Alaska

Betty at Alleghany General Class of 1942 Reunion

Tauck Tour group below Zermatt, 1992

*Betty on the dock
at Boppard, Rhine
cruise ship behind*

*Betty in
Liechtenstein*

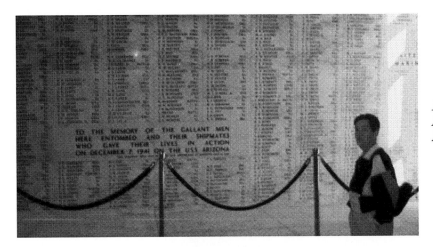

Betty at the Arizona Memorial, Oahu, Hawaii, 1993

At Hawaii Volcanoes National Park

With friend at a luau, Hawaii

~17~

POINT BRITTANY, 1993–1995

Betty and Jack got to meet many of their new neighbors in building two at Point Brittany very quickly. The Fassetts' condo was on the sixth floor (the building had ten floors with ten units per floor except on the tenth floor which had two "penthouse" units) and consisted of a kitchen, a living room/dining room, two bedrooms, two baths, and a large sunroom with a sweeping view of the waters and small islands bordering Tampa Bay. On a Sunday morning after closing on their purchase, but some days before they planned to move into the condo, Betty and Jack decided to perform some preparatory tasks. During the course of using a power drill to install another towel rack in one of the bathrooms (at a place where one would not normally expect to encounter a pipe), the drill pierced a water pipe and water spewed out. Before Jack succeeded in locating a security person to shut off the water to the part of the building served by the pipe, water was several inches deep in the Fassett unit and seeping through the concrete floor to the units below. It took a couple of days to clean up the mess, but the neighbors were gracious (the couple immediately below, who suffered most of the damage, became good friends), and as a result of the necessity of removing much of the wall-to-wall carpeting, Betty got the new berber carpeting she had desired sooner than planned.

Before getting fully settled in the new condo, Betty and Jack had planned a visit to Lora and Parker in Seattle, and they decided to expand that visit to add a tour of the Canadian Rockies. Having been impressed by their initial Tauck Tour, they booked an eleven-day venture with it commencing in Seattle in late July. During the visit with the Masons before commencement of the tour, Parker drove them to Mount St. Helens to view the devastation of that eruption and to visit the recently opened National Park Service visitor center. They also attended a band concert in the center at the locks on the canal where one can view salmon running up the waterway in spawning season. Another day, they traveled east to visit one of Washington's wineries and to sample its product.

Upon joining the tour group in the lobby of a downtown hotel, Betty and Jack were pleasantly surprised to see Loretta and Andy Chau, who had decided to join the Fassetts for the tour. The tour coach proceeded northward to catch ferries to and from Whidby Island, one of the San Juans, and then to Vancouver where the beautiful gardens at Queen Elizabeth Park were wandered before settling in a hotel. The following day, a small group opted to board a seaplane for an interesting flight to a landing outside of Victoria where the equally magnificent Butchart Gardens were in bloom. There the New Brunswick Parliament building and other historic sites were visited. After traveling up the coast in the coach, with a midday stop for lunch at an Indian village, the group spent a night at the modern ski resort in Whistler. Then, heading east across the mountains and over the upper Columbia River, the group stopped for a night in cabins at beautiful Emerald Lake. Following a morning of wandering trails along the lake, the coach again headed northward on Columbia Icefields Parkway to Jasper Park. While most of the group were housed in the main lodge, which contained the dining room, during the two days in Jasper, the Fassetts and Chaus stayed in a separate lodge next to a rapid stream. It had a huge fireplace and conference room as well as two large bedrooms. A photo below the head of a large deer mounted above the fireplace bore a plaque commemorating the fact that Britain's sovereigns had stayed there during a Canadian visit in 1939. The mounted deer undoubtedly had been a local since, during their stay in the lodge, the Fassetts and Chaus saw an abundance of deer and moose wandering the grounds and bathing in the stream.

From Jasper, the coach returned south on the parkway with a stop for a tour of the Athabasca Glacier before arriving at Chateau Lake Louise for one night and two nights at the famous hotel in Banff. The scenery throughout was spectacular, and the Fassetts had another pleasant surprise when they went to their assigned room in Banff. Andy and Loretta had informed the tour guide that the date was the Fassetts' wedding anniversary, and the assigned room was the bridal suite, complete with flowers and chilled champagne. At the evening dinner, the orchestra leader offered congratulations, and the musicians played the anniversary waltz. It was very moving! Finally, on to Calgary for the Chaus and Fassetts to catch the first flight of their return by way of Phoenix to Point Brittany.

Once well-settled in the senior community, Betty and Jack became involved in many of its activities. A large group of men and women, led by resident volunteers, assembled each morning at the main swimming pool behind the clubhouse for an hour of exercise in the water. Betty shortly became a regular member of the group and eventually a substitute leader when needed. When a computer instructor was hired to provide a series of classes in basic computer skills, both Betty and Jack attended the classes, but they did not acquire their own computer until several years after moving to Point Brittany. At the first annual meeting of Building Two's condo association after their arrival, Jack was elected treasurer for the ensuing year. After two years in that position, he became president of the association and filled that post until the annual meeting preceding the Fassetts' departure from Florida. Since the association established the budget each year and thus the level of residents' fees, the monthly meetings of the association were generally well-attended. Issues such as the level of reserves appropriate to cover future major expenses, the levels of insurance coverage, or the need for special assessments for such purposes as painting the building, replacing the roofing, or repairing the bulkheading, brought lively debates.

The residents of Point Brittany supported an active social life within the community. The large clubhouse, with a library, a room with pool tables, several card rooms, and a large ballroom, as well as locker rooms with exercise facilities and saunas for both sexes, was an active center. There was a monthly schedule of early evening dances (bring your own bottle and snacks) with an amazingly talented dance band made up of retired musicians from the area. Both men's and women's clubs had monthly noon meetings featuring a variety of speakers, including many local politicians seeking the votes in such a community.

The Fassetts' second year at Point Brittany coincided with the fiftieth anniversary of the Normandy landings. Betty and Jack planned a European trip but decided to forego returning to either Britain or France where many veterans were going for the many planned observances. Instead, they joined another Tauck Tour, this time to Spain and Portugal, which started in Lisbon on June 5 (allowing viewing of the Normandy festivities the following day on TV at the Hotel Tivoli Lisboa, their headquarters in Lisbon). The capital of Portugal was an intriguing city located on the Tagus River where a large memorial to the many Portuguese explorers responsible for making so many great discoveries was located. The group visited the ancient cloisters and monastery, the Coach Museum (displaying a variety of ancient horse-drawn vehicles), and St. George's Castle as well as the more recent earthquake memorial and statue of Columbus. However, some of Betty's and Jack's most memorable experiences came during the two afternoons they had free time to wander the city on their own. They browsed through Commerce Square on the waterfront and rode a cog railway to the upper portion of the city where there were narrow streets and laundry lines spanning most of the streets and alleys.

Crossing the suspension bridge over the Tagus, the coach took the group (a full load with thirty-eight tourists, a guide, and the driver) to the old town of Sintra to tour the fourteenth-century royal palace, returning to Lisbon through Estoril, a resort town. Subsequently, the coach proceeded south to the Algarve coast, the country's foremost Atlantic Ocean coastal resort area, passing through heavy forests including some groves of Portugal's famous cork trees. The final night in Portugal was spent in the very modern Hotel Quinta Di Lago, from which Betty and Jack spent their free morning wandering the white sand beach. Crossing into Spain the following day, the coach left the coast and reached Seville and the very picturesque old Hotel Alfonso XIII, with its statues, fountains, courtyards, but very modern guest facilities. After the day of traveling and a hearty Spanish dinner, it was challenging to stay awake while attending a show that featured lots of flamenco dancing.

The tour was separated into small groups the next morning to travel by horse-drawn carriages through Maria Louisa Park. In the afternoon, Betty and Jack wandered through the old Jewish Quarter, the Plaza de Espana, and the imposing Seville Cathedral. En route from Seville to Algeciras, the tour's quarters for its visit to Gibraltar, the group visited Jerez, the center of Spain's sherry production for a tasting of its wine. Then, along the Straits of Gibraltar, the African continent was viewed across the water. After the formalities of being allowed to enter, the Rock was an intriguing adventure with its rugged terrain, deep tunnels, and profusion of Gibraltar apes—really amazingly friendly monkeys who were everywhere. After lunch at the Rock Hotel, the group proceeded along the Costa del Sol to the resort town of Marbella. By coincidence, their arrival occurred at the same time as an annual religious festival involving an impressive evening parade that Betty and Jack watched as they returned from strolling the boardwalk along the Mediterranean.

Before arriving for their final few days in Madrid, the group headed inland and spent nights in Grenada (main attraction: Alhambra Palace), Cordoba (a city with heavy Moorish influence including Mezquito Cathedral), and Almagro, staying in the Parador, a former convent, built in 1596 (the town is on the Plain of La Mancha and it was an important milestone on the route followed by Don Quixote as related by Cervantes). They also stopped in Toledo to visit the Church of San Tome where El Greco's *The Burial of Count Orgaz* is a tourist attraction. Unlike the other Spanish cities visited, Madrid is a thriving, modern city, and Betty and Jack enjoyed wandering through the marketplace and down the wide avenues except when they decided to explore a government building on the Paseo de Castellano and, as they approached the entry, two military men with drawn submachine guns blocked their way (it was a time of heavy security due to Basque separatist terrorist attacks). Needless to say, the Fassetts retreated quickly. The final day in Madrid was spent with the group visiting the Royal Palace and the Columbus Memorial before consuming the entire afternoon in the Prado. Following the usual farewell cocktail party and dinner with effusive speeches at the Inter-Continental Hotel, the group disbanded and went their separate ways to the airport and their destinations (only one other couple was from Florida; most were from New York or California).

With the mid-1994 publication of *New Deal Justice*, lengthy and thoughtful reviews of the book began to appear in Kentucky's media beginning with the *Ashland Independent* on Sunday, September 25 . Having long aspired to write a biography of Chief Justice Vinson (also a Kentuckian), the reviewer praised Jack's "labor of love in his resting years." The *Bowling Green Daily News* of Sunday, October 29, described the book as "well-written, well-documented and meticulously done," but the *Kentucky Post* of Covington review headline commented "length weakens New Deal Justice." It concluded that "a book half as long would be of value to the nonlawyer." The *Madisonville Messenger* of November 16 noted that "this is the first definitive biography of the Reed life and with the voluminous footnotes and indices we may not need another"; the Sunday review in the *Lexington Herald-Leader* by a Louisville lawyer questioned "whether Reed merits a full-scale biography," but concluded that "Fassett's biography certainly captures the essence of the subject." This spate of Kentucky reviews (later ones appeared in the *Journal of Supreme Court History*, the *American Historical Review*, and the *Yale Survey of Current Legal Issues*) awakened Kentucky Wesleyan College (which Stanley Reed had attended in Winchester before it moved to Owensboro) to the fact that the justice, who had essentially been forgotten, was probably its most distinguished alumnus. As a result, the College declared April 18, 1995, "Stanley Reed Day," commissioned a bust of the justice to be dedicated that day, and invited Jack, whose book was featured in the February edition of *Today*, the college's publication for alumni and friends, to give an evening address at the college. Since a Kentucky bookseller with several stores in the Lexington area also invited Jack to appear for book signings, Betty agreed that it was an ideal opportunity to see some parts of the Bluegrass State not previously viewed on their several hasty trips across the state. Accordingly, after enjoying the hospitality of the college and appearing at the bookstores, the Fassetts visited Sousa's "Old Kentucky Home" and several historic sites in Frankfort. They then followed the Kentucky

Bourbon Trail from there past a number of famous distilleries to the Maker's Mark Historic Site, one of the oldest still-operating distilleries in the country. Offered a tour (but no samples except for bourbon-filled chocolates), Betty enjoyed sticking her finger in one of the huge, wooden fermenting vats.

Later in 1995, the Fassetts took their last European land tour with Tauck. Called "Classic Italy," the group met, after overnight flights from New York, in Rome's airport on June 3 and for fourteen days traveled the length and breadth of Italy, starting with a drive past the Bay of Naples and Mount Vesuvius to the resort town of Sorrento. There the coach-load of tourists were allowed an afternoon to sightsee or to recover from their travel before the usual introductory reception and dinner. The next morning, the group experienced a ride along the spectacular Amalfi Drive with its sheer, unguarded drops to the Tyrrhenian Sea. There were fabulous views of seaside villages. The coach stopped in Amalfi to visit its cathedral, downtown, and waterfront. The group enjoyed lunch at a villa high on a lemon-grove-covered hillside in Revello. Returning to the ancient Grand Hotel in Sorrento, Betty and Jack took its outdoor elevator to the Bay of Naples waterfront and wandered the docks and beach. The third day was spent visiting the ruins of Pompeii, which had been buried by the eruption of Mount Vesuvius in AD 79, but has been excavated and tells a grim but intriguing tale of life at that time. The group departed from Pompeii in time to check into Hotel Majestic Roma, located near the U.S. Embassy on Via Veneto, in time for another big Italian dinner. During three days in Rome, the group was constantly on the move visiting the seemingly endless attractions of the City of Light: Vatican City with its Sistine Chapel and museum; St. Peter's Basilica and Square; Trevi Fountain; the Roman Forum and the Coliseum; ruins of the Imperial Palace and Circus Maximus; the Spanish Steps; and much more. Late afternoon of the third day, the coach took the group to an inn in the Frascati Hills for another sumptuous meal and an opportunity to view the pope's summer palace at Castelgandolfo, returning to Rome after dark. Visits to Ovieto, Torgiano, Assisi, Spello, and San Gimignano consumed four busy days. The climb from the town and the museum in Assisi to St. Francis Basilica was definitely worthwhile, and the visit to Torgiano was highlighted by wine tasting at the region's wine museum. After visiting Pisa with its cathedral and leaning tower, the group stayed at an Italian Riviera beach resort in Forte Dei Marmi where Betty and Jack walked the white sand beach and toured the beautiful gardens. Taking a short train ride from Spezia, a small contingent of the group traveled to the Cinque Terre villages, inaccessible by car since high on cliffs overlooking the sea. Betty and Jack hiked the cliff walk at Manarola before taking a train back to Vernazza where they had reservations for lunch at a restaurant high on a cliff with a fine view of the many small boats in its harbor.

The final lap of travel in the coach was an early morning trip to Florence where the group checked into the ancient-outside, but modern-inside Hotel Brendleschi in the heart of the city. Following a lecture on the many sights of the city, the group visited the Academia to see Michelangelo's *David* and then had the next day and a half free to visit their choices of attractions. Betty and Jack chose to visit the Uffizi, St. Croce Church, to dine with another couple at a small restaurant on Via delle Oche, and to visit the shops and spectate the activities on the Ponte Vecchio over the Arno River. After considerable cogitation, Betty chose an attractive multicolored gold necklace at one of the jewelry artisans' shops, and Jack obtained the required documents for declaring the purchase at customs and for obtaining a refund of the VAT (value-added tax) upon exiting Italy.

Bidding farewell to their driver at the Florence railroad station, the group boarded a fast train for Venice. From the Venice terminus, the group was transported by canal boat to the Hotel Europa & Regina located on one of the major canals, a bridge away from St. Mark's Square. During the final two days of the tour, the group visited the Basilica of St. Frari and the Ducal Palace and took a boat trip to Murano for a demonstration of glass making. On the final evening, in groups of four, rides were taken on one of Venice's famous gondolas, poled by a standing guide, through many of the canals of the city. During the adequate free time allowed for tour members to choose their own activities, Betty and Jack wandered St. Mark's Square, visited the Rialto market and the Academy Gallery, and sat on a bench watching traffic on the Grand Canal.

Departing the hotel early in the morning on the final day for the boat ride to the Venice airport, the Fassetts encountered an unexpected adventure. They were booked on an Alitalia Airlines flight to Rome and a Delta Air Lines flight from Rome to New York, but a strike by Alitalia's crews had grounded its planes, making it impossible to make the Rome connection. An unsympathetic Alitalia agent suggested that the Fassetts either return to their hotel to await the end of the strike or take a train to Rome to catch another flight home. In desperation, Jack importuned a Lufthansa agent to stop one of its flights already taxiing to depart for Frankfurt and to book the Fassetts on two open first-class seats so they could catch a Delta flight with available seats from there to New York. In Frankfurt, a German custom agent stamped the documents needed to obtain the VAT refund and Jack placed the envelope bearing Italian stamps provided by the jeweler in an airport mailbox. Despite these factors, in due course, Jack received a credit for the tax refund on his credit card.

Only a matter of days after returning from Italy, Betty and Jack were departing from Tampa Airport, but heading west this time. Expecting their first child at summer's end, Lora and Parker had rented a large house at Sun River Resort in Bend, Oregon, for a week in July and invited all of the Fassetts and Mermins to join them there for a reunion/vacation. The Maryland and North Carolina contingents flew to Portland and drove rented cars to Sun River. Betty and Jack flew to Seattle and enjoyed a scenic ride through Washington's agricultural region (buying and eating ripe cherries en route) and crossing the Columbia River at the Dalles on the way to Bend. At Sun River, the group (including very pregnant Lora) played tennis every day, took numerous hikes, and the more adventurous ones climbed a mountain and rode a raft down the rapid-flowing river. The most exciting day for Betty and Jack was a trip to Crater Lake, where a boat ride was taken to a small, steep, heavily wooded island in the middle of the lake. Having received a promise that they would be picked up in an hour on the boat's next trip, the group went ashore for a hike. However, shortly thereafter, a lightning storm developed, and all boat trips were suspended for several hours, stranding the group on the island. In the interim, Parker, Caleb, and William slid on their bottoms down an icy central crater, and Parker and William even dove, very briefly, into the icy lake. On the return trip to Seattle, Parker detoured for a visit to Mount Hood, where skiing and skateboarding were observed and lunch was eaten in the lodge.

Since it had been arranged that Betty would attend Lora for the arrival of her anticipated daughter, Betty and Jack flew back to Seattle in early September. However, since Darby did not arrive until almost three weeks after the scheduled due date, Betty and Jack had a good visit with the eager parents during the wait. Parker, who normally took an early morning trot around Green Lake before departing for work, altered his routine and played tennis with his father-in-law at the Green Lake courts most mornings instead. While Betty and Lora waited, Jack cruised all of the many used-book stores in Seattle, finding a number of very welcome additions to his again-expanding Supreme Court collection. After Darby arrived on September 27, Betty had a fine time displaying her nursing skills with her first female grandchild, and she returned to Point Brittany happy with the accomplishment of the mission.

Views of Point Brittany from the bay. LEFT: *Jack, David and Betty.* RIGHT: *Gunnar, Joy and Connie.*

Morning exercises in the pool

Betty reading in Jack's library chair

Canadian Rockies Trip

UPPER LEFT: *Betty at Butchart Gardens, Victoria Island*
MIDDLE LEFT: *Betty in front of cabin at Jasper*
MIDDLE RIGHT: *Hiking at Lake Louise*
LOWER LEFT: *With Loretta and Andy Chau at Whistler*

Trip to Portugal and Spain

UPPER LEFT: *Betty before Memorial to Discoverers, Lisbon*
RIGHT: *Plaza de España, Seville*
LOWER LEFT: *Plaza Major, Madrid*

Trip to Italy
UPPER LEFT: *Betty holds up the leaning tower of Pisa*
UPPER RIGHT: *On the road to Amalfi*
LOWER LEFT: *With Michelangelo's David*
MIDDLE RIGHT: *At the Coliseum, Rome*
LOWER RIGHT: *San Marcos Square, Venice*

UPPER LEFT: *Jack, Betty, Caleb, Joy, Mimi, William and Jack, Jr. at Duke Gardens*
UPPER RIGHT, MIDDLE LEFT: *Stranded at Crater Lake*
MIDDLE RIGHT: *Jack, Lora and Betty at Mt. Hood*
LOWER RIGHT: *Darby joins the Fassett clan*

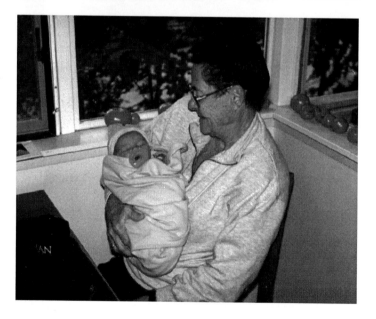

⤳18⤲

Point Brittany, 1996–1999

After the somewhat taxing year with the Italian venture and the western trips, Betty was happy to relax for a few months. Having decided they were getting to be too old for European land tours, she and Jack discussed with their travel agent the possibility of a longer trip on a liner for the summer of 1996. Two events intervened, but did not alter their plan. First, the Redins decided to sell their home on Tierra and join the Fassetts at Point Brittany. It thus became even more routine for the foursome to have cocktails and dinner together on a regular basis, and Connie joined Betty as a regular at the morning pool exercise sessions. Gunnar also quickly found himself involved in condo politics at building three, where they had bought a unit, so he and Jack found themselves on the overall Point Brittany governing board together.

The captain of Jack's Lakewood tennis team and his wife, Bob and Jean Parker, were longtime residents of the Redins' new location, and Jean still worked as a travel agent. In early March, Jean excitedly announced to the Fassetts and another tennis-team couple that she had just been offered an irresistible deal. The special deal occurred because Royal Cruise Line was selling its flagship, the *Crown Odyssey*, to Norwegian Cruise Line, with the vessel to be delivered in Fort Lauderdale, Florida. Since the Odyssey had been cruising in the Pacific, in an attempt to fill the vessel on its trip to Florida, a previously unadvertised cruise from San Diego to Florida at a deeply discounted rate was offered. To make the offer more attractive, a series of evening shows and dances were scheduled for the cruise. They featured Russ Morgan's Orchestra and were called "a tribute to the big bands." Betty and Jack and Tom and Kate Avirett signed on to join the Parkers on the cruise, and all booked flights from Tampa to San Diego to arrive for the March 15 sailing.

Except for the fact that the first three days in the Pacific were very rough, it was a restful and exciting cruise. A large proportion of the passengers became sick during the rough weather, the dining rooms were only sparsely populated, and barfing bags were profusely placed in obvious places throughout the ship. The

Parkers and the Aviretts were all indisposed, but, amazingly, despite her fear of the sea from her Atlantic crossings of WWII, Betty had no problem and she and Jack didn't miss a meal, regularly used the exercise room, and saw several movies and each of the evening shows en route to Acapulco. In that scenic resort, they took a tour of the homes of movie stars, visited the Peace Chapel with its cross of peace, and watched daring divers swan dive off Quebada Cliff 149 feet into the surf below. After three more days at sea, by which time the Pacific storm had abated and the sailing was smooth, the *Odyssey* reached Balboa, the Pacific terminus of the Panama Canal, and waited its turn to begin traversing the Miraflores and Pedro Miguel Locks, the Gaillard Cut, and Gatun Lake. Then the ship cleared the Gatun Locks and Limon Bay before entering the Atlantic Ocean. Betty and most of the ship's passengers spent several hours on deck observing the operations during the dramatic passage of locks going from ocean to ocean. The calm, final three-day trip to Florida was interrupted only by a stop (requiring ferrying to shore) at Isla San Andres, a remote island owned by Colombia, but with no memorable features.

Upon their return, following their plan, Jack opted to book a cabin on Holland-America's M.S. *Maasdam* for a two-week cruise to Scandinavia and Russia. Sailing from Devon, England, on July 22, the Fassetts were met by cruise staff at Britain's Gatwick Airport and taken by coach for boarding at a pier not far from the white cliffs of Dover. The Baltic cruise was very relaxing, a pleasant change from the frequent suitcase packings, early morning risings and departures, and rigidly fixed schedules of most land tours. The first two nights and the whole first day were spent sailing the North Sea to Oslo, Norway, allowing time to explore the ship's many amenities, enjoy great meals, and attend one of the evening performances by the talented cast of young entertainers. While conveniently docked in Oslo, Betty and Jack took a walking tour to see the neoclassical Royal Palace, the Sculpture Park, and the Kon-Tiki Museum before returning to the ship for the return transit of the Oslofjord and a short open-sea voyage to Arbus, Denmark, where the Fassetts chose only to take a stroll through the old town.

After a short sail through Denmark's narrow channel to the Baltic port of Warnemunde, Germany, a large proportion of the Maasdam's passengers boarded a train for a visit to Berlin, a couple of hours away. Having previously toured that city, Betty and Jack took a brief hike around Warnemunde and then enjoyed a leisurely afternoon on shipboard. Since their cabin had a veranda, it was not necessary to leave the cabin to repose and watch outside activity either at sea or in a port. The following day was spent at sea as the ship sailed north to Stockholm, Sweden, where it docked in a channel some distance from the city. Betty and Jack opted to hike into the city and then spent several hours walking the streets of Old Town and visiting the Royal Palace and the Stockholm Cathedral. At the next port, the following day, the ship was able to dock a short walk from all of the sights and activities of Helsinki, Finland. While the Fassetts viewed many historic buildings, they were more intrigued by the large, open-air market where all kinds of flowers, food, attractive items of clothing, and all sorts of other merchandise were offered for sale. St. Petersburg, Russia, was a short sail up the bay and the Neva River from Helsinki. Because the ship was moored at a commercial dock some distance from the city, and for security reasons, the group was escorted in coaches to all of the sights during the two days in Peter the Great's capital city. At the Cathedral of St. Peter and St. Paul, Betty and Jack viewed the tombs of many czars and their families; they viewed the golden dome of St. Isaacs and resisted the temptation to buy various items from black-market hawkers who dogged the tourists trying to sell their merchandise; they saw a ship moored on the Neva, the *Aurora*, where the Russian revolution began; and they spent half a day touring the immense Hermitage with its famous collections of art and artifacts. St. Petersburg to Copenhagen was the longest journey of the cruise, again consuming one whole day plus two nights. It provided extra time to enjoy the ship's exercise room, one of its hot tubs, and to attend both a movie and an evening show as well as to sample the food at some of the specialized cafes. During a day in Copenhagen, before flying home from there, a group walked from the mooring to the square of the Royal Palaces, had the mandatory glimpse at the unimpressive Little Mermaid in the harbor, and spent the evening witnessing many activities at Tivoli Gardens. The return flight, as was the flight out, was direct to Tampa without the usual connection problems, so the Baltic trip received a top grade from Betty.

The spring of 1997 brought the end of Jack's commuting to New Haven (and of his accumulation of frequent-flyer miles and receipt of director fees) as he retired from the board of UI. Betty joined him for the final trip and for the UI dinner at the Lawn Club where he was presented with a silver platter engraved with the signatures of all of the other board members. He had already retired in March 1996 from the New Haven Savings Bank board, at which time he was presented with a framed artist's rendition of the bank's headquarters building, facing New Haven's central green, with a plaque commemorating his thirty years of service as a corporator and trustee of that institution. During the 1997 visit, Betty and Jack stayed with Andy and Irene Wong in their showcase-modern home on Sleeping Giant in Hamden, as they had on a number of prior visits to New Haven after they ceased to have the apartment in Madison Towers. The Wongs, as was their custom, feted the Fassetts with a dinner at Betty's favorite Italian restaurant in Connecticut, with a group of old Lawn Club cronies. Betty had always favored Italian cuisine, and that liking had been enhanced during her tour of Italy.

In anticipation of their fiftieth wedding anniversary in 1997, Betty and Jack had booked an early summer cruise from Venice on the new flagship of the Holland-American fleet, M.S. *Rotterdam VI*, scheduled to make its maiden voyage then. Upon receiving notice that the launching would be delayed (and given special credit toward a subsequent trip), the Fassetts checked with Tauck Tours, and it had room for another couple in a group scheduled to tour southern Texas, a state the Fassetts had crossed several times, but which they had never toured. The group assembled at the airport in Dallas and immediately departed for Galveston, from where they spent a couple of days touring its sights and visiting the Gulf Coast before traveling south to Corpus Christi, where they stayed at an attractive beach resort. After traversing an expanse of ranching country, the group spent two nights in a restored old hotel in downtown Laredo, from which Jack and Betty walked across the border to Mexico's Nuevo Laredo, with its persistent hawkers of drugs and other commodities. En route to San Antonio, there was a bus ride though a wild animal sanctuary where a friendly giraffe actually tried to stick its head through an open bus window. During several days in San Antonio, the group, of course, visited the Alamo and its museum, traveled to several buildings outside the city dating to the days of the Spanish occupation, strolled the attractive River Walk which ran past the tour's hotel, and enjoyed a meal atop the revolving tower on the fairgrounds. En route to Austin, the group visited Lyndon Johnson's ranch, notable for its prolific pecan trees. In Austin, the attractions were the university and the

Lyndon Johnson Library, which contained an interesting collection of memorabilia and many audiotapes from Johnson's presidency that were available for listening.

Returning from Dallas to Point Brittany, Betty and Jack prepared to celebrate their golden anniversary at a family gathering planned by their children. Several days prior to the big day, they flew to Manchester, New Hampshire, where they were met as they exited their flight by Darby, presenting two caps embossed with crossed tennis racquets and inscribed "FASSETT FIFTIETH—1997." The Masons transported them to Waterville Valley, a winter ski resort, where Parker had arranged for weeklong rentals of two spacious ski lodges to accommodate the Fassett clan. There were nearby tennis courts where interfamily matches were played every day, a variety of hiking trails, and bicycles for rental, which some of the group rode around the area. Mimi took a class in fly fishing given by an instructor beside a mountain stream, and Parker, William, and David even went swimming in that cold water. With a short ride to Snow's Mountain, the group all rode a ski lift, which permitted fine viewing of the mountainous area. Darby became intrigued by the signs along the road announcing "Moose Crossing," and she subsequently sent her grandmother a replica of one such sign, which still is attached to her refrigerator door. On August 4, the group drove into town for a private dinner at the Mad River Tavern, and the children presented Betty and Jack with a leather-bound album commemorating the event. It contained copies of numerous photos of the celebrants; a lengthy essay entitled "All We Ever Needed to Know about Marriage We Learned from Watching Jack and Betty Play Tennis"; another document entitled "A Numerology of 50 Years Together," which, among other computations, reported that the marriage had lasted 18,263 days, involved purchase of twenty-five new automobiles, and survival of one plane crash. Philatelist-son Jack contributed a sheet of special U.S. postage stamps bearing Betty's and Jack's likeness, and Mimi had arranged for a card from the White House, signed by Bill and Hillary Clinton, congratulating Betty and Jack on the occasion. Somehow the producers had found and reproduced the card Jack had given to Betty on their first anniversary, which had predicted "When our hair has turned to silver, and our anniversaries gold . . . I'll still be proud as heck, sweetheart, You're mine to have and hold." The first item in the album was an eight-stanza poem entitled "The Ballad of Betty and Jack" which commenced:

Oh, do you remember sweet Betty Conrad?
In 1947 she married our dad.
They hadn't much money —t'was after the war—
But they'd plenty of love, and big dreams, that's for sure.

It concluded:

Now it's been 50 years since 'twas their wedding day,
And their kids and grandchildren gather round them to say
Thanks for your love and your dreams and your care.
May fifty more years you together both share.

Among the wedding mementos presented that night was even a copy of the August 4, 1947, edition of *Life* magazine. The following night, the group celebrated Joy's forty-eighth birthday with a dinner in one of the lodges, plus games and songs.

In December, to share Darby's first Christmas as a Santa believer, Betty and Jack again flew to Seattle. Most prior Christmases, starting at Old Orchard Road and continuing on to Tierra, most of the family had convened in the seniors' homestead to celebrate the holidays, but that routine had dwindled as the grandsons grew older and, on a couple of years, Betty and Jack had traveled to Chapel Hill for Christmas. After the holidays in 1997, a heavy snowfall hit the Northwest, bringing traffic to a standstill in Seattle. On the day the Fassetts were scheduled to depart, the Masons' steep front street still had not been plowed, and the radio was warning that traffic was not moving at the airport. However, since the Fassetts were anxious to return to Florida, Parker braved the continuing storm in his four-wheel-drive vehicle and got them to the airport where, after two de-icings of the wings after they boarded, the Fassetts' plane was one of the few to succeed in taking off that night.

One of the reasons Betty and Jack wanted to get back was that they wanted to prepare for their rescheduled cruise on *Rotterdam VI*. It no longer was the new vessel's maiden voyage, which had sailed from Venice, but a rescheduled cruise to the Black Sea which departed from Civitaveccia, the port of Rome. Greeted at Rome's airport, within a few hours they were settled in their cabin and the cruise had commenced. The Fassetts rested and enjoyed the view as the sparkling ship proceeded along the coast of Italy for a day, passing through the Strait of Messina between the boot and Sicily, and then entering the open Mediterranean to a first stop in Keflion at the tip of the Greek peninsula. After a sightseeing trip there to view the deep-cut canal across that peninsula, the ship arrived at its first major port, Kusadesi, Turkey. That port permitted the tourists to spend most of a day touring the intriguing Roman ruins at Ephesus and to visit the shop of a Turkish carpet merchant who described how the hand-made rugs were produced and had an assistant unroll an increasing pile of examples of the art.

After navigating the Dardanelles, the ship docked in Istanbul and served as the base for several days of touring that city and its environs. Highlights were visits to the Blue Mosque, St. Sophia's Church (built by Constantine in AD 325), Topkapi (ancient residence of the Ottoman sultans), and the noisy, but interesting, Grand Bazaar, where Betty enjoyed watching some of the haggling over purchases and wandering through some of the adjacent shops. Proceeding into the Black Sea, the ship next docked at Yalta in the Ukraine (along the coast called the Black Sea Riviera) to allow a visit to the hillside palace at Livada where Stalin, Churchill, and Roosevelt convened in the closing days of WWII. Many celebrated Russian artists and writers (including Chekhov, Tolstoy, Tchaikovsky, and Rachmaninoff) once sojourned in the area, which contains many mansions, beautiful parks, and several museums. After Yalta, there were sightseeing stops in Odessa, also in Ukraine, Costanza in Romania, and Nessabar in Bulgaria, before again traversing the Dardanelles. From Costanza, a number of passengers opted to take a daylong trip to visit Bucharest, Romania's capital, but Betty and Jack chose to rest in the comfort of the liner because Betty was feeling quite fatigued after all of the activities.

The final port on the trip was at Piraeus, the port of Athens, from which it was a scenic ride to a hotel in that city. A day touring the city at their own pace allowed time for Betty and Jack to visit the Acropolis, the Temple of Athena, and the Parthenon, as well as to view the Agora and the Olympic Stadium built for the first Olympics in 1896 at the location of the original site built by Lycurgus in 330 BC.

Returning from Athens, the second reason Betty had been anxious to return home from the holidays in Seattle came to the fore. For several years, her normally exuberant energy had waned, and she was having an increasing loss of feeling in all of her extremities. Her primary physician ultimately referred her to a neurology specialist who, after performing extensive nerve tests, concluded that she was suffering from CIDP (Chronic Infectious Demyelinating Polyneuropathy), a progressive disease for which the only effective extant treatment to stem the advance was regular intravenous injections of a gamma globulin. Before many weeks of that treatment, at another visit to her primary doctor, he had an echocardiogram performed. Upon viewing the results, the doctor immediately called St. Petersburg's Bayfront Hospital to prepare a bed for Betty with an admission diagnosis of a blood clot to the heart. Jack rushed Betty to the hospital, and an able, youthful (he still ran marathons) cardiologist, who had treated several of the Fassetts' friends, was summoned to evaluate the patient. He astutely recognized that the problem was not a clot, a not uncommon diagnosis, but a heart tumor (a myxoma), a condition he and other Bayfront doctors had viewed on autopsies, but had never treated in a live patient. He promptly contacted the area's leading heart surgeon (who, coincidentally, was a tennis player, and he and his wife were social friends of Betty and Jack) who directed that surgical removal of Betty's myxoma be the first procedure on the operating room schedule for the following day.

Removal of the myxoma was a particularly challenging operation since it not only occupied a large part of the heart's left atrium but extended into the ventricle and interfered with the proper operation of the valve. The operation involved almost identical procedures with a heart transplant: a mechanical device for circulating blood while the surgery on the heart was performed; a long incision in the chest wall and a movement of ribs to reach the heart; however, rather than removing the heart, the myxoma was removed through incisions in the right atrium and the septum (dividing the chambers) with the incision of the septum being repaired with a graft from the pericardium. The operation took several hours, during which time Jack was accompanied by surgeon Andy Chau, his tennis partner, and they were kept informed of progress by a surgical nurse who brought them reports and also photographs taken of the offending large myxoma. After a couple of days in intensive care, Betty spent three weeks recovering in the hospital. The doctors had hoped the period would be less, but, on one day, her heart stopped beating, requiring electrical shock treatment to restore the beat. Moreover, some days into her recovery, Betty suffered a TIA (transient ischemic attack), suddenly losing her ability to speak and control of one side of her body because of a blood clot reaching the brain. She was rushed to the magnetic imaging machine for a viewing of the disturbed area of the brain and additional drugs were given, but fortunately the disturbance cleared spontaneously without any permanent damage.

All of the children were in Point Brittany during the crisis, and a major topic was Betty's care upon release from the hospital. Prior to the CIDP diagnosis, Jack had been seriously considering purchasing the second large penthouse unit in Building Two (the Chaus occupied the other similar tenth-floor unit), which was about to come on the market and was much larger than the Fassetts' current unit (plus having a large cherry-paneled den with abundant bookshelves). Under the changed circumstances, Betty and Jack decided it would be more prudent for them to move to a full-service retirement home having a clinic and a nursing facility as well as independent living units. After several months, during which Betty progressed from walking a few feet on their condo balcony to walking with Jack for extended distances along the Point Brittany waterfront, the Fassetts began visiting some of the many full retirement communities in the St. Petersburg and Bradenton areas. They had about decided on a waterfront community in St. Petersburg when Joy and Paul visited and presented strong arguments for first evaluating several similar facilities in the Chapel Hill area. The result was a weekend of scheduled visits to Carol Wood, Carolina Meadows, and the Forest at Duke and an unscheduled visit to the still-under-construction Croasdaile Village in Durham operated by United Methodist Homes. Since the latter offered a unit squarely meeting their desires plus a close proximity to, and relationship with, Duke Hospital and its physicians, Jack signed an agreement to join the community before returning to Florida.

Betty's first airline travel following her amazing recovery from her operation had occurred in May, 1999, prior to the Chapel Hill trip. Several months earlier, Wes Poling, the president of Kentucky Wesleyan, visited the Fassetts to advise that his Board of Trustees had voted to award an honorary doctor of laws degree to Jack at the next graduation ceremony and to invite Betty and Jack to stay with him and his wife, Carol, during the days of the ceremonies. Flying to Evansville, Indiana, Betty and Jack rented a car and took the pretty ride over the Audubon Highway to Owensboro and enjoyed their stay in the lovely old mansion on the college campus which served as the president's home and a center for entertaining. After being effusively honored at the outdoor graduation ceremony and feted at a large dinner party in the president's home, Betty and Jack returned directly to Florida. During their flight home Betty joked that Jack had now become a double-doc since Yale had, some years earlier, retroactively converted the bachelor of laws degree it had awarded in 1953 into a doctor of jurisprudence degree.

Jack and Betty took one additional not-too-taxing trip from Point Brittany before moving to North Carolina. For many years, Jack's younger sister, Mary Lee, had been desirous of convening a Fassett family reunion. During the summer of 1999, she and her husband reserved for a week a facility on a lake in Lakeville, Connecticut, designed for such occasions and summoned all of the clan. They all came, including cousins from California and their children, and it was an invigorating week of storytelling, reminiscing, tennis games, boat rides, some golf, lots of hiking, and much conviviality. Betty, of course, was unable to join any of the vigorous activities, but she enjoyed entertaining the youngsters and sitting in the sun by the swimming pool. Connie and Gunnar joined Betty and Jack on the flight to the reunion. Their plane landed on Long Island and they spent a couple of nights visiting the Redins' son, Eric, and his family in Dix Hills. Before taking the ferry ride across Long Island Sound to Connecticut, the Fassetts and elder Redins took a ride in their rental car to the end of Long Island, visiting East Hampton and stopping at the cemetery where Connie's and Jack's parents and grandparents are buried, the old homestead where she and Jack were born, and the high school they both attended. Returning to Point Brittany, Jack became deeply engaged in packing for the move to North Carolina.

Crown Odyssey Cruise through the Panama Canal
ABOVE: *Betty viewing the canal*
RIGHT: *Peace Chapel and Cross of Peace, Acapulco*
BELOW: *With the Parkers and Aviretts at dinner aboard ship*

Jack before the Royal Palace in Oslo

Betty at the open air market in Helsinki

Betty at the Square of the Royal Palace in Copenhagen

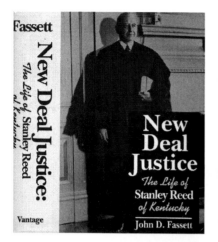

Kentucky Wesleyan Events

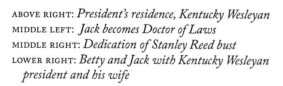

ABOVE RIGHT: *President's residence, Kentucky Wesleyan*
MIDDLE LEFT: *Jack becomes Doctor of Laws*
MIDDLE RIGHT: *Dedication of Stanley Reed bust*
LOWER RIGHT: *Betty and Jack with Kentucky Wesleyan*
  president and his wife

*Dining with Redins
in Building 3*

*On the shuffleboard
court with Jeff*

*An affair at the
Point Brittany Club*

50th Anniversary Group at Waterville Valley, 1997

Farewell Party at Point Brittany, 1999

~ 19 ~

CROASDAILE VILLAGE, 1999–2005

Croasdaile Farm, named after a location in Wales by its owner, was once a very large dairy farm located in the northwestern part of Durham County, only about a mile from the new college campus being built for Duke University after it was endowed by the Duke family. As the university campus grew to include a constantly expanding medical center, the owners of the dairy farm thoughtfully converted the fields and forests into a large, multiuse development. One part became the Croasdaile Country Club, with a championship golf course; another, an area of retail stores, commercial offices, and multifamily apartment buildings; and most of the land was devoted to a well-planned development of high-level residences. However, a prime, 110-acre plot adjoining a park area and a large pond (created by damming the small stream that bisected the property) was made available to United Methodist Homes, a not-for-profit organization of the United Methodist Church. That organization, for some years, had operated a retirement home in a nearby more-urban setting primarily for aged Methodist ministers and their wives, begun at a time when persons in that profession rarely had retirement plans.

By the summer of 1999, when Joy took her parents to see Croasdaile Village, construction of the attractive, countrified community was almost complete, and residents had just begun moving into the 71 cottages and 186 apartments (96 two-bedroom; 63 one-bedroom; 37 studio) in the Homestead building, designated as independent-living units. In addition to those and the large commons encompassing an auditorium, library, game room, gift shop, branch bank, post office boxes, and large dining room, all reached through a large reception room, the community had separate buildings attached by covered walkways containing a large nursing facility (114 beds) plus separate dementia-treatment and assisted-living facilities. Part of the financing for the construction of Croasdaile Village was provided by Duke University, and at the outset it was anticipated that the Duke Medical Center would utilize part of, and cooperate in staffing, the Croasdaile medical facilities. There was no religious test for admission to the community, and while the residents were predominantly Methodists and included a number of former ministers, the community included some Catholics and Jews and a great assortment of other believers, and even some doubters.

By the time Croasdaile Village opened, all of the units had been sold (residents had no ownership rights and their initial payment was amortized over fifty months, but they had some assurance of lifetime occupancy) and there was a waiting list, but Betty and Jack avoided a wait because the purchasers of the unit they were shown and liked on the top floor of Homestead were procrastinating, and then changed their minds, about moving in. Since the Fassetts were prepared to move into the completed unit promptly, without requiring alterations, their offer to join the community was accepted.

Unit A354 consists of an entry, a small kitchen, a large room that comprises the dining area and living room, and two bedrooms, each with its personal bath designed for senior citizens. The living room has a wall of windows overlooking the campus, with a view of the southern cottages and the pond. Jack and Betty had recently purchased a large-screen TV with a bookcase unit to house it. Those items and Jack and Betty's two reclining chairs fit nicely in the area next to the windows. All of the walls of one bedroom were required to accommodate the oak bookshelves and their contents (Jack's Supreme Court book collection) which were moved from Point Brittany. There was ample room for writing and computer desks in each of the bedrooms.

Prior to her parents' move to Croasdaile Village, Joy had made inquiries among medical friends and had made appointments for Betty with recommended cardiology and neurology specialists at Duke. As part of the admission process to the retirement home, Betty and Jack both received complete medical evaluations from the staff doctor and a physician's assistant at the home and, being pleased with those medicos and the clinic facilities, they decided to use them as their primary physicians. Upon Betty's first visit to the cardiologist at Duke, Jack commented to him about the uniqueness of a patient surviving a myxoma and Dr. Cahliff responded that it was, indeed, unusual, but that at Duke they saw an average of one new myxoma patient a month since patients were sent there from throughout the world for diagnoses and treatment. That reassured the Fassetts that they had made a wise decision in moving to Durham. Betty's new neurologist initially ordered a continuation of the gamma globulin treatments administered in Florida, but he ultimately concluded that her primary problem was Parkinson's disease, so he discontinued the intravenous treatments and attempted to control the neurologic symptoms with other drugs.

Despite her physical limitations, Betty promptly became an active participant in the activities at Croasdaile Village. Upon the Fassetts' arrival, a member of the rehab staff at the home was conducting an hour of exercises, primarily in chairs, in the auditorium each weekday morning for any residents who wished to participate. Betty immediately became a regular attendee. Within a couple of months, the leader left for another position, and Betty became the temporary substitute. When chairs and equipment were installed in a large, lower-level exercise room with a mirrored wall and nearby locker rooms, Betty continued to be the leader of the 9:30 a.m. session five days each week, with only one long intermission in late 2000 plus two shorter ones subsequently when she had cataract operations on both eyes, until she was no longer able to carry on in 2006. In view of Betty's dedication to the activity, for her eightieth birthday in December

2001, Jack and her children contributed funds to permit Croasdaile to purchase all of the exercise room equipment (which had previously been leased at substantial cost) and, at a heavily attended celebration on her birthday, a plaque was installed formally naming the facility the Betty Fassett Exercise Room. Since the plaque disclosed the year of Betty's birth, Betty ever after pointed out that she could never fool anybody regarding her age.

The intermission in Betty's leading exercises beginning late in 2000 resulted from another medical crisis. In accordance with normal procedure, Betty was sent by the Croasdaile clinic to a Durham X-ray lab for a mammogram about a year following the Fassetts' arrival at the home. When the X-ray disclosed a problem in her left breast, Betty underwent a biopsy that showed the presence of cancer cells. The doctors strongly recommended a full mastectomy and removal of the associated lymph nodes, and Betty and Jack regretfully accepted that advice. As she was awaiting her scheduled date for surgery, the Fassetts received a call to inform them that Betty's mother, who had been in a nursing home in Pittsburgh suffering from Alzheimer's disease, had passed away at age ninety-nine (Betty's father had died suddenly while the Fassetts still lived on Old Orchard Road). Accordingly, the week before Betty entered the hospital for her mastectomy, the Fassetts, with Joy along sharing the driving with her father, made a speedy trip to Pittsburgh and attended the funeral.

In a nod toward democracy, from the outset, Croasdaile Village organized into a number of separate neighborhoods, each with a representative to a Residents' Council. Although it had no actual power over finances, personnel, or other administrative matters, the council did oversee the operation by residents of the gift shop, had input with respect to activities, and, through many committees, enhanced the convivial atmosphere in the community. While Jack was a member of the small committee that drafted the original by-laws for the association and he served on the nominating committee for officers the first few years, he had had his fill over the years of being active in organizations and he declined any other role in the association. He did make a contribution at the organizational meeting of the third-floor south neighborhood group: when his neighbor, who was presiding, asked for suggestions for a name for their neighborhood, Jack, recalling the condo he had almost purchased in Point Brittany, suggested "Penthouse South," and that name thereafter stuck.

Missing his heavy Florida tennis schedule, Jack was interested in resuming his participation in that sport, so he explored the availability of nearby facilities. Senior tennis activities at the Croasdaile Country Club were very limited, so Jack chose initially to enter several USTA-sanctioned seniors' tournaments (in the seventy-five-plus category) in the area. As a result, he qualified for the state championships held in Charlotte in September 2001, and Betty accompanied him to that multiday event. It was a well-run affair and Jack was doing well until, enjoying a substantial lead in his third match, a blood vessel in his calf ruptured and he had to default. The Fassetts hurried back to the clinic at Croasdaile Village, where he received treatment. While that event convinced Jack to terminate playing in singles tournaments, he was most fortunate shortly to be introduced to a former neighbor of one of Betty's bridge friends who was an equally ardent competitor and was a member of the Faculty and Staff Tennis Club of the University of North Carolina in Chapel Hill. Jack fit in comfortably with several groups, mostly of retired academics and administrators, at that club, and he was able completely to fulfill his exercise and competitive desires thereafter. His new friends at the Farm (the land on which the tennis club had been constructed had once been a farm) elected him an honorary member of the club. For several years, while the club fielded a team playing in an interclub doubles league, he played on that team. In that way, he got to visit most of the other tennis clubs in the Research Triangle area.

At the outset, Betty's physical activity at Croasdaile was limited to the exercise room. Later, for help with her Parkinsonism, she also attended rehab classes conducted by members of the Croasdaile staff. In addition, she became part of a bridge group that required frequent mental activity. One attribute of retirement homes is that they provide lots of opportunities to play bridge or other games. In addition, the activities director, together with the residents' supporting committee, scheduled many afternoon and evening talks and musical performances by individuals or groups available to perform before large, appreciative audiences. Some of the lecturers were residents, and within the first few years, Jack was tapped several times to discuss the operation of the Supreme Court and to describe his experiences in the electric industry. The established rule with respect to such sessions was that they last no more than an hour and the evening sessions always commenced at seven o'clock, in order not to conflict with bedtimes. Several able Durham-area groups (for examples, a chorus composed of employees of SAS Institute in Research Triangle; and a local company of talented Gilbert and Sullivan light-opera singers) offered shows that residents looked forward to every year. Even the talks by local medical people, lawyers, and politicians drew large audiences. Initially, Croasdaile Village had two in-house TV channels that broadcast notices of scheduled events, resident's birthdays, daily menus, weather information, and other administrative information. After a few years, an additional channel was added so that performances in the auditorium and monthly presentations by the home's executive director could be shown.

In addition to live performances, the Activities Committee scheduled showings of movies in the auditorium on most weekend evenings. Betty and Jack preferred to watch their choices of films from one of the movie channels provided by the home's cable-TV hookup while reposing in their recliners, but that routine was altered when, after a significant number of residents complained about the content or quality of some of the films shown in the auditorium, that committee appointed Jack the designated movie critic for the home. Before being scheduled to be shown in the auditorium, Betty and Jack would have a private viewing of each film and Jack would write a short review warning of any offensive content and commenting on the quality of each proposed movie. Initially, the films viewed were on VCRs, but later the committee obtained them from Netflix and they were DVDs. Four, and sometimes five, evenings each week, Jack would start a DVD at 7:00 p.m. and Betty would retire when the movie was completed and Jack would compose his one-page review before retiring. During the years this routine was followed, Betty and Jack reviewed well over a thousand films. Before moving to Croasdaile Village, Betty had often stated that she had rarely seen any movies since Jack was always too busy to go while working and too busy writing books in his retirement years in Florida. That deficiency was certainly not present in the retirement home.

During the first few years at Croasdaile Village, Betty and Jack, in addition to their short trips to Pittsburgh and Charlotte, made car trips to Kiawah Island and to visit their son and his wife in Washington

Grove, Maryland. The Kiawah trip was occasioned by the rental there by Lora and Parker of a condo for two weeks during a summer. While Betty's Parkinsonism precluded her participating, Jack got to play a lot of tennis with Lora, Parker, and the father of a family, also with two children of ages similar to Darby and Sylvie, who the Masons knew from their days in Charlotte. Betty enjoyed the beach and the sightseeing with the youngsters, and the Masons and Fassetts enjoyed some excellent seafood at restaurants on Kiawah and Seabrook islands.

The visit to Washington Grove had multiple purposes. In addition to visiting their son and his family, they visited the Women's Memorial to WWII veterans where they entered Betty's name in the computer and saw her military history reported, and they also attended grandson William's graduation ceremony from Montgomery Blair High School. They also visited Arlington National Cemetery, observed a service at the columbarium, and discussed with an administrator arrangements for the eventual placement together in the columbarium of their own ashes. They were inspired to take the latter action by the fact that, on the death of the husband of one couple with whom they dined frequently during their first years at the home, the widow, who had been a navy nurse, ran into complications in making arrangements for his interment in Arlington.

Betty and Jack attempted only two trips by air subsequent to moving to the home. The first one occurred in 2003 when Holland-America Line offered a special rate for small groups to the Fassetts since they had become Mariners as a result of their prior cruises. For years, the Fassetts had discussed introducing the Redins to the pleasures of cruising and, when they agreed to join in a Western Caribbean cruise, Jack's younger sister and her husband also opted to join the group. Since the M.S. *Veendam* sailed from Tampa, Betty and Jack flew there and spent a couple of days on either end of the enjoyable cruise with the Redins at Point Brittany. In calm, sunny weather, the ship sailed south with stops at Key West and Grand Cayman Island before heading west for stops for shopping at a port in Guatemala and at the resort island of Cozumel in Mexico before returning to Tampa.

The second flight in 2004 was made to Buffalo, New York, where the Fassetts were met and driven to the famous Inn at Lake Chautauqua. The occasion was the fiftieth anniversary of the historic school segregation decisions by the Supreme Court, and the entire affair was sponsored by the Robert Jackson Foundation. In addition to participating, with three other 1953-term law clerks, in a forum about the development of the decisions (the forum was recorded and aired over C-SPAN on two succeeding Saturday nights), Betty and Jack participated in numerous meetings and discussions during their three-day stay at the interesting old center for summer intellectual events. One noon, Betty and Jack dined with the sisters who were involved in the *Brown* decision, and Linda Brown invited the Fassetts to attend the scheduled dedication of the historical site in Topeka, Kansas, commemorating the event. At Croasdaile, Jack prepared a large display (much of it consisting of books from his Supreme Court collection), which occupied the cabinets in the reception room, to celebrate the anniversary of *Brown v. Board of Education*. He also presented a lecture relating to the decision. The Chautauqua trip was the Fassetts' last attempt to travel by air (they never got to Topeka, but Joy did visit the memorial and brought souvenirs of her visit to her father) because they found it necessary, in view of Betty's instability, to use wheelchairs going through the airports, and the traveling was not comfortable.

Betty had obtained her own Dell computer shortly after arriving at Croasdaile, and she greatly enjoyed using it to send e-mail, play solitaire, make greeting cards, shop, and do research regarding medical matters. Jack had a Mac on which he primarily kept records, did email, writing, and financial reports, and occasionally explored the used-book market for volumes still missing from his collection. As Betty's Parkinsonism advanced, she found using the computer quite frustrating, even with modifications made by Mimi (an administrator in the Montgomery County, Maryland, library system and knowledgeable about computers) and a representative of the state agency for the disabled whom Joy had contacted.

Early in their Croasdaile residency, Betty and Jack were asked to become members of a Heritage Committee, whose primary function was to raise endowment funds for the community. While the original plans for the home had included a separate chapel, that amenity was deleted for financial reasons, and a major objective of the Heritage Committee was to raise sufficient funds to build the chapel. As a result of many contributions, including one from the Fassetts, that goal was accomplished, and a most attractive and functional interfaith chapel was completed in 2004. While on that committee, Betty and Jack also endowed the private dining room outside the main dining hall set aside for small gatherings of residents and their families or meetings of modest-sized groups. Betty and Jack became very interested in the backgrounds and aspirations of the many young people working in the dining room, mostly recruited from local high schools by Morrison's Dining Services, the operator of the dining room, and in 2002 Jack created a fund to provide scholarships of one thousand dollars each to applicants among those young people who were going on to further education. During the first few years, two scholarships were awarded each year. There was considerable joy and satisfaction in watching the progress of recipients, many of whom came back to visit during college breaks.

In addition to regular visits from members of the family, many of whom stayed with and were entertained by Joy and Paul in their Chapel Hill home, a number of old friends found their way to Croasdaile Village to the delight of the Fassetts. Andy and Loretta Chau visited, and Jack arranged a tennis match for the old partners against friends at the Farm. Russell Eustice, the adjutant of the 134th Evacuation Hospital, stopped to deliver to Betty a copy of the monograph cited in chapter 2. During the visit, it was discovered that Russell was a Colgate University classmate and friend of Jack's high school football coach. As a result, for a period, Jack received communications from his old coach who had retired in Hamilton, New York, the home of Colgate. However, the coach and his wife were never able to make the trip to Durham he proposed. Mary Jane and Keith Zimmermann, who had retired to a senior community near Asheville, North Carolina, visited twice in 2004, but under less pleasant circumstances since Keith had been referred to the Duke Cancer Center for treatment of that disease. Unfortunately, the treatment was not effective and, upon Keith's demise, Mary Jane moved to Colorado to be near their daughter. Both Rusty Hart and Ray Rapp had died before the Fassetts left Florida, and both of their spouses passed on within a few years without a chance for reunions with the Fassetts. Until her Parkinsonism made use of her computer too taxing, Betty regularly exchanged emails with two of her tennis team cohorts from the Lakewood Club in St. Petersburg, both of whom had been widows for several years. A surprise visit in 2003 from one of Jack's protégés at

UI, who had recently retired after a number of years as CEO of the company, allowed Jack to learn about events at his old company and in NEPOOL, but Betty and Jack have not returned to New Haven since his retirement from the board in 1997. Joy and Paul do visit Connecticut for annual reunions of the Mermin family, so Betty and Jack receive some reports regarding the major changes in the New Haven area.

A major social event at Croasdaile each day is the dinner meal in the expansive dining room. From the first, Betty and Jack ate early, occupied the same table for four, and welcomed an alternating group of other couples to join them. Unfortunately, but not surprisingly since becoming accustomed to losses is a necessary part of being a resident of a retirement home, by early 2005 each of the seven most frequent sets of dinner companions was reduced to a single member (five widows and two widowers). In that year, a further major expansion of Croasdaile Village had begun (fourteen additional cottages and fifty-nine new independent-living units in a greatly expanded Homestead), which involved large increases in the size of the kitchen and the dining room and addition of a cafe to add new services. In compliance with a request because of dining space constraints during construction, Betty and Jack volunteered to move their dinner hour even earlier (4:30 p.m.) and thereafter they opted to dine without dinner companions on most occasions when Betty was up to dining in the dining room.

With all of the family planning to be in the Durham area for the year-end holidays in 2005, Lora reserved the banquet room at Croasdaile Country Club (where her wedding reception had been held) for a party featuring an open bar and dinner and invited all of Jack's Chapel Hill tennis friends and their wives. It was a festive affair with many toasts and a few speeches, and Lora and Joy followed that celebration by writing to everyone on the Fassetts' Christmas card list (obtained from Betty) requesting responses marking Jack's eightieth birthday. Lora had obtained personalized postage stamps bearing a photo of her father as a nude baby (found in her grandmother's photo album), which she employed for the solicitation. To his pleasure and amusement, Jack was inundated with messages, including a couple of humorous essays and a clever poem from two of his tennis friends from Florida.

Croasdaile Village
ABOVE: *View of Homestead from pond*
MIDDLE LEFT: *Dining area of Fassett unit*
MIDDLE RIGHT: *Living room and TV area*
BELOW: *Betty in Croasdaile pool with Connie*

Dedication of Betty Fassett Exercise Room 2001
LEFT: *Presentation by Chairman and Executive Director of home*
MIDDLE LEFT: *Poster by family*
MIDDLE RIGHT: *Betty and Jack with refreshments*
BELOW: *Betty dons tee-shirt*

*Redins, Wilbers and
Fassetts depart for the
Carribean, 2003*

FAR RIGHT:
*Ground-breaking for
the new chapel*

MIDDLE, BELOW:
*Ribbon cutting for
Fassett Dining Room*

ABOVE: *Betty with Masons in Duke Gardens*
MIDDLE LEFT: *Swimming with Darby*
MIDDLE RIGHT: *Feeding Sylvie*
BELOW: *With Jack, Mimi and William at William's high school graduation*

FORUM AT CHAUTAUQUA, 2004

Participants (four 1953-Term law clerks seated)

Luncheon with Cheryl and Linda Brown

Jack's 80th Birthday celebration
assembled at Croasdaile Country Club, December 2005

Ode to Jack Fassett

There was a good gent from St. Pete,
Whose tennis – to watch – was a treat.
It was not fun to play him
Just ask Dick or Jim.
'Twas his wish to leave all badly beat.

Point Brittney and Lakewood were sites of his play.
He preferred these surfaces: har-tru or clay.
His serve was a patsy; his backhand a flop,
His net play was streaky and his drop shots didn't drop.
So how on earth did he keep winning day after day?

The secret, of course, was his legal trained mind
Which allowed him a weakness in each game to find.
He'd poke away at the victim with all of his might
And keep his opponent at bay well into the night.
Through all of his training, he never learned to be kind.

As he moved up in years, doubles more was his game.
With Andy it brought him some national fame.
Some mornings brought matches with Hallin and Goad
For the Doc and the Lawyer, they were a manageable load
Except on those days when the older gents went lame.

One sad day indeed he moved north to the hills
To find new opponents who took potions and pills.
We are told now he is eighty
And that's very weighty
Now he huffs and he puffs as he kills!

Toward ninety he now sets his sights.
With Betty, family and memories he delights.
But the racquet still gathers no dust
To the courts most days still a must
Much like Ben Franklin felt with his kites.

We are certain his birthday will rock
Regardless of the time on the clock
For Jack, the celebration is a treat
A gift from all he has beat
Here's to the lawyer, the writer – the jock!

With warm wishes,
Dick & Jim

ABOVE: *A birthday envelope with celebratory stamp*
LEFT: *One of the tributes which arrived in a specially-stamped*
envelope for the actual birthday, January 30, 2006

~ 20 ~

CROASDAILE VILLAGE, 2006–APRIL 22, 2008

Fully a year prior to the completion in 2007 of construction of the new additions to the facilities at Croasdaile Village, Betty's heart, which had been monitored closely since her arrival in Durham, began to malfunction and add to the problems caused by her Parkinsonism. Her Duke neurologist and cardiologist had prescribed a number of drugs in efforts to improve her neurologic and cardiac conditions, but the heart problem continued to deteriorate. She was sent by the Croasdaile clinic to the emergency room at Duke Hospital on October 6, 2006, from which she was admitted to the Heart Center with a diagnosis of congestive heart failure. At the Heart Center, her condition was stabilized with diuretics and other drugs, and she was released after five days for a week of additional monitoring in the Pavilion, Croasdaile's nursing facility. In view of her situation, Betty finally had to relinquish, after having led the exercise sessions for almost six years, her role as exercise leader. Not long thereafter, Jack also relinquished his role as movie critic for the community.

With limited activity and careful monitoring of the many prescription drugs prescribed for her complicated ailments, Betty was still able during 2007 to play bridge, watch some movies, listen to book tapes, struggle with her computer, and enjoy occasional trips to Chapel Hill for get-togethers with Joy's family and family visitors, who stayed at Joy's. However, the Fassetts had to forgo a trip to Providence, Rhode Island, in April to join the rest of the clan attending the wedding in the Brown Atheneum and reception in the Brown Faculty Club of grandson Caleb and Lydia Haile. They also had to miss William receiving his diploma and Phi Beta Kappa key from their alma mater, the University of Rochester, later that spring.

On August 4, 2007, an exciting family get-together in Chapel Hill occurred on the occasion of Betty and Jack's sixtieth wedding anniversary. Joy arrived to pick up the celebrants (routine for several years for such trips since Jack avoided driving after dark and after having a cocktail) in her car with a painted sign on the rear window proclaiming "Just Married—60 Years." The ride from Croasdaile to Chapel Hill was amusing since many passing vehicles honked their horns and waved to "the newlyweds."

As 2007 ended, Betty felt so poorly that she and Jack never composed or sent an annual holiday-greetings letter to their rapidly decreasing list of old friends or even to their list of extended family members. Nevertheless, they enjoyed hearing from the few surviving members of their North Haven social group, and from some of their old Isla, Tierra Verde, and Point Brittany friends and several generations of the Fassett clan. They also enjoyed receiving a card in early 2008 announcing the celebration by Irene and Andy Wong of their sixty-fifth anniversary at their retirement home in Hawaii. However, that was soon followed by a communication from Dot McVay from Sun City, Arizona, announcing the death of Jerry, thus leaving Betty and Jack the last surviving couple of their old North Haven bridge club and New Year's Eve party gang.

With the opening of the new Croasdaile Village Cafe, Jack was able conveniently to obtain dinners for Betty and himself each evening for serving in their apartment. Betty did go to the dining room on a few special occasions (a friend's ninetieth birthday, visits by Connie and Gunnar and son Jack and Mimi) using her new wheelchair for the trip and at the dining table. The Redins still resided in St. Petersburg, but they had moved to a retirement home there similar to Croasdaile Village from where they came for a visit to Betty and Jack. Betty also attended the presentation in 2007 to dining room employees of nine scholarships pursuant to Jack's program. The fund was enhanced that year both by Jack and by contributions from a couple of other residents to permit awards to the larger group. She joined Jack in feeling great satisfaction in watching the progress of the young recipients.

In the second week of 2008, Betty's heartbeat became very rapid, and the fibrillation that had been noted on EKGs since her operation in 1998 became much more pronounced. As a result, her cardiologist had her admitted once again to the Heart Center at Duke with the goal of remedying the problems. The plan was to perform a cardioversion (an electric shock treatment designed to cause the heart to revert to normal rhythm). Prior to that procedure, a transesophogeal-echocardiogram was performed to view the heart and attempt to assure that no extant blood clots would complicate the procedure. Betty was released from the Heart Center two days after the cardioversion with her heart in normal rhythm, but within hours after returning to Homestead her heart was beating wildly and her blood pressure dropped to a very low level. Not desiring, as proposed by the summoned medics, to return immediately to the emergency room at Duke Hospital, Betty chose to be treated in the Pavilion where her cardiologist and the Croasdaile medical staff were able to stabilize her condition, but not to reduce the rapid beat or eliminate the flutter.

After ten days in the Pavilion and a brief stay in Homestead, Betty was readmitted to the Duke Heart Center, and a second course of treatment was undertaken to attempt to correct her rapid pulse and cardiac flutter. This time, rather than employing electrical cardioversion, a regimen of the drug Tikosyn, which also required a preliminary transesophogeal-echocardiogram and three days of close monitoring of the effects of administration of the drug by the doctors in the hospital, was undertaken. With hopeful results during the hospital monitoring, Betty was permitted to return to her apartment for continued monitoring by the Croasdaile clinical staff, but, much to the distress of Jack, Betty, and her cardiologist, Tikosyn ceased to be effective after only a few days and the rapid beat and fibrillation returned.

Following a full discussion of Betty's condition with her cardiology specialists, and recognizing that her existing condition both severely limited her functioning and was life threatening, Betty agreed to return a third time to the Heart Center to permit consideration to be given by those specialists (particularly the electrophysiologists) to performance of an ablation (a cauterization) of the disruptive chamber of her heart and implantation thereafter of a pacemaker to attempt to assure that the beat did not become too slow. However, because of Betty's having had open-heart surgery in 1998 (for removal of the myxoma), the specialists at the Heart Center were most reluctant to attempt those procedures and, following another electrical cardioversion, she was started on a regimen of daily doses of the drug Amiodarone along with supporting daily doses of blood thinners (originally Lovenox and Coumadin, but, after a week at home, only Coumadin).

The first few weeks following Betty's return from her third Duke Heart Center session of 2008 were both challenging and stressful. She had developed a very troublesome eye infection while in the hospital, which required frequent visits to her ophthalmologist and to a retinologist and applications of drops three times every day. She also had signs of internal bleeding, which also caused concern and required additional treatments. Her new wheelchair was used for her frequent trips to the clinic, where blood samples were regularly taken to monitor the condition of her blood and pulse and blood pressure readings were also taken. The wheelchair was also used for appointments with other doctors. She used her walker for all of her activity in the apartment. During her first three weeks home, though, she had three bad falls in the apartment, two of which occurred on weekends and required summoning of emergency medical assistance. The falls resulted in large hematomas on her arms and legs, and one caused a bleeding lip, a tender nose, and a fractured upper dental plate. As a result of these occurrences, the doctors concluded in early April that the risks arising from the Coumadin, even after the dosage was reduced, outweighed its benefits in concert with the Amiodarone, and discontinued further administration of that blood thinner.

In the two weeks after the Coumadin was discontinued, Betty's condition greatly improved. Her hematomas largely disappeared, no other bleeding occurred, she did not fall again (even greater care having been taken in the use of the walker and resisting any unusual movements), and she felt and slept better than when she first returned home. The regular monitoring of her vital signs and her blood continued, and the Amiodarone allowed her to continue to maintain an acceptable heart rate and rhythm. Betty began receiving treatments in the apartment three times a week by members of the rehabilitation clinic, and the goal was to begin soon having those sessions at the rehab center. Since the beginning of Betty's hospitalizations in January, Jack suspended his trips to the Farm for his tennis games, but both of his groups continued playing with substitutes and awaited his return.

While Betty and Jack have not yet resumed their program of watching movies for the Activities Committee, Betty did get to watch and enjoy most of the 2008 NCAA basketball tournament games for both men and women. The Masons visited from Seattle, and Betty and Jack greatly enjoyed socializing with their fast-growing granddaughters, Darby and Sylvie, and their parents. The Masons, Mermins, and Betty and Jack had a fine mini-reunion during the Saturday night of the Masons' visit at Joy's home in Chapel Hill, with Darby, Sylvie, David, Lora, and Joy all displaying their prowess at a video dancing game.

In short, conditions improved and optimism prevails!

60th Wedding Anniversary
ABOVE: *Leaving Croasdaile in decorated "limo"*
MIDDLE LEFT: *Arriving at Joy and Paul's*
MIDDLE RIGHT: *60 tennis balls*
BOTTOM LEFT: *Anniversary pies*

Scholarship Presentation Ceremonies
2006–2007

Jack Fassett presents
award to Tierra Collins.

Caleb and Lydia's wedding – Providence 2007

Paul, Joy, Jack and Mimi at Caleb and Lydia's wedding